BENJAMIN FRANKLIN

BENJAMIN

FRANKLIN

A Perspective

By Louise Todd Ambler

An exhibition held at the
Fogg Art Museum
Harvard University
Cambridge, Massachusetts
April 17 through September 22, 1975

COVER ILLUSTRATION: NO. 41   Benjamin Franklin by Augustin de Saint Aubin after a drawing by Charles Nicolas Cochin, the younger.

FRONTISPIECE: NO. 36 Mezzotint of Benjamin Franklin, by Edward Fisher after the painting by Mason Chamberlin.

This exhibition and catalogue were organized with the aid of a grant from the National Endowment for the Arts in Washington, D. C., a Federal agency.

© Copyright, 1975, by the President and Fellows of Harvard College. Permission to reproduce any portion of this catalogue must be obtained from the Fogg Art Museum.

Library of Congress Catalogue number 75-3512

Typesetting and printing by Thomas Todd Co., Boston.
Design by Lance Hidy, Cambridge.

Contents

Illustrations	6
Foreword	8
Acknowledgments	10
Introduction by I. Bernard Cohen	13
Chronology of Benjamin Franklin	17
Benjamin Franklin: A Perspective by Louise Todd Ambler	21
Notes	104
The Catalogue	108
Bibliography	145

Illustrations

4. *The Art of Swimming* . . ., frontispiece and title page	26, 27
6. *Poor Richard . . . an Almanack* . . . 1752, September	30, 31
9. *La Science du Bonhomme Richard* . . ., title page	33
10. *M. T. Cicero's Cato Major* . . .	34, 35
11. Portrait of Benjamin Franklin by Robert Feke	38
Portrait of James Bowdoin II by Robert Feke	39
12. *Proposals Relating to the Education of Youth* . . .	40, 41
14. Portrait of John Winthrop by John Singleton Copley	46
15. Small reflecting telescope made by James Short	47
17. Portrait of Edward Holyoke by John Singleton Copley	49
18. Master of Arts diploma conferred on Benjamin Franklin	50
19. Letter from Franklin to Thomas Hancock, 11 Sept. 1755	52
19. Subscription form, signed by Franklin, 11 Sept. 1755	53
19. Draft for subscription, signed by Franklin, 11 Sept. 1755	54
21. Virgil's *Æneis*, printed by John Baskerville	57
22. Letter from Joseph Mico to Thomas Hubbard, 13 May 1758	114
23. Letter from Franklin to John Winthrop, 10 July 1764	59
24. Large reflecting telescope made by James Short	61
25. Meridian telescope made by John Bird	62
26. *Two Lectures on the Parallax* . . ., by John Winthrop	115
27. Letter from Franklin to John Winthrop, 11 March 1769	116, 117
28. *The Young Gentleman and Lady's Philosophy* . . .	64, 118
29. Weights and pulleys made by Benjamin Martin	65
30. Electrostatic machine attributed to Benjamin Martin	66
32. Orrery made by Benjamin Martin	67
33. Bust of William Pitt by Joseph Wilton	68
34. *Experiments and Observations* . . ., 1769, James Bowdoin letter	71
36. Mezzotint of Franklin by Fisher after Chamberlin	FRONTISPIECE
40. Medallion of Franklin by Jean-Baptiste Nini	79
41. Engraving of Franklin by St. Aubin after Cochin	80

42.	Medallion of Franklin by Jean-Baptiste Nini	81
43.	Medallion of Franklin by Jean-Baptiste Nini	82
44.	Portrait of Franklin by Joseph-Siffred Duplessis	83
46.	Bust of Franklin after Jean Jacques Caffiéri	84
47.	Bust of Franklin after Jean Antoine Houdon	84
48.	Bust of Franklin, Sèvres porcelain	85
49.	Bust of Franklin, silver	85
50.	Statuette of Franklin after François Marie Suzanne	86
51.	Statuette of Franklin identified as "General Washington"	86
52.	Miniature of Franklin after Anne Rosalie Filleul	87
53.	Engraving of Franklin by "N. L. G. D. L. C. A. D. L."	88
54.	Medallion of Franklin by Wedgwood	91
55.	Queen Charlotte Sophia by Wedgwood	126
56.	King George III by Wedgwood	127
57.	Doctor Joseph Priestley by Wedgwood	73
58.	Granville Leveson-Gower, Marquis of Stafford by Wedgwood	128
59.	Sir William Hamilton by Wedgwood	128
60.	William Eden, Lord Auckland by Wedgwood	130
61.	Lady Auckland by Wedgwood	130
62.	William Pitt by Wedgwood	130
63.	Thomas Pitt, First Baron Camelford by Wedgwood	130
64.	Charles Pratt, First Earl Camden by Wedgwood	132
65.	Mrs. Elizabeth Montagu by Wedgwood	132
66.	Viscount Richard Howe by Wedgwood	133
67.	Sir Joseph Banks by Wedgwood	96
68.	Dr. John Fothergill by Wedgwood	133
69.	Sir William Herschel by Wedgwood	135
70.	Benjamin West by Wedgwood	135
71.	David Garrick by Wedgwood	135
72.	James Tassie by William Tassie	136
73.	John Tassie by James Tassie	136
74.	Edmund Burke by William Tassie	137
75.	Adam Smith by James Tassie	138
76.	David Hume by James Tassie	138
80.	Portrait of George Washington by Charles Willson Peale	93
82.	Portrait of John Adams by John Singleton Copley	95
84.	Portrait of James Bowdoin II by Christian Gullager	98
85.	The Slave in Chains by Wedgwood	99
86.	Portrait of Thomas Jefferson by Gilbert Stuart	100
88.	Drawing for a memorial to Benjamin Franklin	102

Foreword

Benjamin Franklin is the first of three consecutive exhibitions on the theme "Memories of Eighteenth-Century Harvard" which the Fogg Museum will mount in commemoration of the nation's Bicentennial. The second will be *Lafayette* and the third *Harvard Divided,* an exhibition that will focus on the division of sentiments between the Patriots and Loyalists who were graduates of the College.

Neither Harvard nor any other college can claim Benjamin Franklin as one of its matriculated students. Franklin tells us in his *Autobiography* that his father, a tallow chandler and soap boiler, apprenticed all his elder brothers to different tradesmen. He had higher ambitions for Benjamin, however. He sent him to Boston's Grammar School when he was eight. His intention was to prepare Benjamin for the ministry. But his father's plans soon changed.

After spending less than a year in the Grammar School, Benjamin writes that his father,

> from a view of the Expence of a College Education which, having so large a Family, he could not well afford, and the mean Living many so educated were afterwards able to obtain . . . altered his first Intention, took me from the Grammar School, and sent me to a School for Writing and Arithmetic . . . where I acquired fair Writing pretty soon, but I failed in the Arithmetic, and made no Progress in it.

The boy's stay in his second school was also short. His father took him from it at the age of ten to assist him in his candle-making business. Thus ended Benjamin Franklin's formal education.

But as Franklin's career and accomplishments prove — if additional proof is needed — there is no predictable correlation between the duration of a young person's formal education and the merit of his or her subsequent intellectual achievements and service to mankind. Franklin's contributions were remarkable in a broad spectrum of areas of endeavor: as an experimental scientist, in encouraging the growth of science in America, and in the political and diplomatic arenas. I. Bernard Cohen points out in his introduction to the catalogue that while the objects exhibited are largely Harvard memorabilia, they allude to the whole range of Franklin's achievements.

Louise Todd Ambler, Curator of the Harvard University Portrait Collection, has devoted several years to delving deeply into nooks and crannies — both physical and historical — to bring to light the story of Franklin's involvement with Harvard. Throughout, her persistence, catholicity of interests, and quiet sense of humor have been worthy of her subject, Franklin himself. To her, to Agnes Mongan whose 1944 exhibition served as a model and whose help is always freely given, to the members of the Advisory Committee, we extend warm thanks.

S. S.

Acknowledgments

During the past two centuries, the Benjamin Franklin memorabilia at Harvard have found their way to repositories throughout the University. Much is kept in The Houghton Library, where Carolyn Jakeman and her assistants in the Reading Room patiently assembled many of the books and documents included in the exhibition. William Bond consented to their loan and, with Roger Stoddard, assisted in the preparation of the catalogue entries.

Other documents required for both exhibition and research were gathered in the Harvard University Archives by Harley Holden and his gracious staff, while the librarians of the Fine Arts Library at the Fogg Museum helped me locate ancient books with quaint call numbers. I am grateful for the assistance and encouragement I received throughout the Harvard College Library system, both in Cambridge and across the river.

David Wheatland and Ebenezer Gay have spent the winter polishing and reassembling the treasures borrowed from the Collection of Historical Scientific Instruments. This is but their most recent effort on behalf of the exhibition, for it is their years of research that have made evident the historical significance of the instruments on display.

Many of the portraits exhibited here usually hang elsewhere in the University. I wish to thank all those who are cheerfully tolerating a bare wall for the duration of the exhibition.

Documents of special interest to the Harvard community have been lent by Mrs. Robert D. Chellis; the American Philosophical Society; the Boston Public Library; Bowdoin College; the Brooklyn Museum; the Rose Art Museum, Brandeis University; and the Massachusetts Historical Society. Their generosity at a time when all items "Bicentennial" are in tremendous demand is deeply appreciated.

Assistance in locating portraits, documents, and elusive facts has come from many individuals: Mona Dearborn and the staff of the Catalog of American Portraits, National Portrait Gallery, Smithsonian Institution; Vivian Scheidemantel Hawes, President, American Ceramics Circle; Gayle Lenihan of The Massachusetts Company, Inc., and Edgar J. Winter, Secretary to the Boston School Committee, who provided information on the Franklin Trust and Franklin Awards.

A generous grant from the National Endowment for the Arts made it possible to bring together the material from these many sources, and to present it in this catalogue and exhibition.

The photographs of objects from Harvard collections were taken by James Ufford and Michael Nedzweski. I wish to thank them and the many others at the Fogg who helped with this catalogue. Linda Ayres attended to myriad details with persistence, patience, and grace.

At the time of this writing the exhibition is not yet installed, but with complete faith that Eugene Souza and his colleagues will get the job done, I offer them now my deepest gratitude.

Louise Ambler

Introduction

Benjamin Franklin's relationship with Harvard College went through four phases. At one time he had thought of going to Harvard and entering the ministry. Later on, while apprenticed to his brother James, he shared the latter's anti-Harvard position, expressed in his newspaper, *The New-England Courant*. This second, or anti-Harvard, phase arose from the fact that Harvard stood for the establishment, notably the party of the Mathers. Thus, the first number of the *Courant* (7 August 1721) announced its "chief design" to oppose "the dubious and dangerous Practice of Inoculation" to prevent smallpox, a new practice that had been introduced at the suggestion of Cotton Mather. It was in the pages of the *Courant* (beginning with the issue of 2 April 1722), as Carl Van Doren noted, that "Benjamin Franklin, sixteen, first speaks in prose known to be his"; he wrote a series of anonymous contributions, slipped under the door of the shop at night, under the pseudonym, "Silence Dogood." One of these compositions was a satirical attack on Harvard College, where "two sturdy Porters named *Riches* and *Poverty*" kept the gate, and Poverty "obstinately" refused entrance to anyone "who had not first gain'd the Favour" of Riches. Learning was enthroned within the temple, but the steps to her high throne made her difficult to reach; most of her worshippers, accordingly, "contented themselves to sit at the Foot, with Madam *Idleness* and her Maid *Ignorance*."

The third phase was Harvard's recognition of Franklin's scientific achievement — the first formal such recognition he gained. It took the form of an honorary degree, an A.M., awarded in July 1753 for having

> made great Improvements in Philosophical Learning, & particularly wth. Respect to Electricity, Whereby his Repute hath been greatly advanc'd in the learned World, not only in Great-Britain, but ev'n in the Kingdom of France also.

Two other colonial colleges followed Harvard's lead: Yale in September 1753 and William and Mary in April 1756; it was not until the end of November 1753 that the Royal Society awarded him its Sir Godfrey Copley gold medal "on account of his curious experiments and observations on electricity." Franklin made his peace with Harvard, and on September 11, 1755 sent an order to his brother John, in Boston, for four pistoles for a book fund for the Harvard library. He had proposed to Thomas Hancock that there be established an annual subscription to provide funds for the purchase of books for the library. His own gift, he wrote, was "but a trifle compared with my hearty good will and respect to the college"; nevertheless, "a small seed properly sown sometimes produces a large and fruitful tree."

These three phases of Franklin's relationship with Harvard are documented in the exhibition, the occasion of this catalogue (NO. 1, the *Courant*; NO. 18, Franklin's A.M. diploma; and NO. 19, Franklin's order to his brother to pay four pistoles for the new fund he had proposed — for some reason Harvard never cashed the order and has preserved the autograph documents in its archives ever since). The fourth and final phase extended over many decades, during which Franklin made gifts of books to the College library (NOS. 13, 21, 35, and 37), oversaw the acquisition of scientific instruments and apparatus (NOS. 24, 25, 29, and 30), and saw to it that Harvard's Professor John Winthrop got an honorary LL.D. degree from Edinburgh in 1771. Franklin performed a most valuable service in helping the College to get the best scientific instruments possible, to replace those lost in the fire of

January 24, 1764. He was then in London as agent for the Pennsylvania colony, and was eminently qualified to act as a scientific advisor.

These links between Benjamin Franklin and Harvard College make it especially appropriate for the Fogg Art Museum of Harvard University to mount a Bicentennial exhibition, the first of three, dealing with Franklin and Harvard. Some thirty years ago, I participated in the preparation of an exhibition at the Fogg, honoring Franklin, Washington, and Lafayette, in which it was seen how Franklin had aided Harvard College in replacing the scientific instruments that perished in the fire: an exhibition assembled by Agnes Mongan. Franklin's warm relations with Harvard in his mature years were made manifest again, five years ago, in an exhibition on Early Science at Harvard. Now, for the third time, Franklin is the subject of an exhibition at the Fogg, assembled by Louise Todd Ambler, who had been responsible for the earlier exhibition of science and scientific instruments. This time, however, Franklin is the sole subject — every possible aspect of his multi-faceted life and career being on display in so far as the resources of Harvard collections permitted (with a bare minimum of borrowings). And, indeed, the astonishing richness of these collections is shown by the very fact that there is no major aspect of Franklin's life and career that is not part of the exhibition. As an aid to the viewer, Mrs. Ambler has not only compiled a catalogue in the usual sense, but she has added thereto a sprightly introduction, in which she has set forth the main lines of Franklin's life and thought in relation to the main topic: Benjamin Franklin and Harvard College. Thus the exhibition and the catalogue are not merely a parochial reminder of the contacts between Franklin and Harvard, but rather use those contacts as an index of the quality of the man and the character of the College and display the whole life and career of Benjamin Franklin in what will be to many a wholly new light.

I. Bernard Cohen
Professor of History of Science

Chronology *Benjamin Franklin 1706-1790*

1706	Born in Boston, January 17 (January 6, Old Style).
1718	Apprenticed to brother James, a printer.
1722	Silence Dogood letters published.
1723	Left Boston for Philadelphia.
1724	Sailed for England.
1726	Returned to Philadelphia.
1727	Junto organized.
1728	Set up printing partnership.
1729	Began publication of *The Pennsylvania Gazette*.
1730	"Took to wife" Deborah Read.
1731	Library Company of Philadelphia founded.
1732	Compiled and printed first *Poor Richard: An Almanack*... (for 1733).
1736	Appointed clerk of the Pennsylvania Assembly; Union Fire Company organized.
1737	Appointed postmaster of Philadelphia.
1740	Invented Pennsylvania fireplace ("Franklin Stove").
1743	Published *Proposal for Promoting Useful Knowledge*, which led to founding of American Philosophical Society.
1747	Communicated results of early experiments with electricity to Peter Collinson.
1751	Academy of Philadelphia opened; *Experiments and Observations on Electricity* published; Pennsylvania Hospital chartered.
1752	Demonstrated identity of lightning and electricity with kite; printed instructions for affixing lightning rods to buildings in 1753 *Almanack*.

1753 Received honorary Master of Arts degrees from Harvard and Yale, and Copley medal from Royal Society; appointed deputy postmaster general of America.
1754 Proposed Albany Plan of Union.
1756 Commanded Philadelphia volunteers on western Pennsylvania frontier.
1757 Sailed for England to negotiate with members of the Penn family; while at sea wrote *The Way to Wealth*.
1758 Selected electrical apparatus for Professor John Winthrop at Harvard.
1759 Received honorary LL.D. degree from University of St. Andrews; travelled in Scotland.
1761 Travelled to Flanders and Holland.
1762 Returned to Philadelphia.
1764 Offered to help restore Harvard Library; returned to London as agent for Pennsylvania.
1766 Testified for repeal of Stamp Act before House of Commons.
1767 Travelled in France; met many French scientists.
1768 Appointed agent for Georgia.
1769 Appointed agent for New Jersey; received thanks of Harvard Corporation for scientific apparatus and bust of Lord Chatham.
1770 Appointed agent for Massachusetts.
1771 Began *Autobiography* at home of Dr. Jonathan Shipley; travelled in Ireland; sent "Hutchinson letters" to Massachusetts Committee of Correspondence.
1773 Published satirical attacks on British policy.
1774 Ridiculed before Privy Council; dismissed as deputy postmaster general; Deborah Franklin died.
1775 Returned to Philadelphia; elected postmaster general by Congress; elected to Second Continental Congress; went to Cambridge with commission to reorganize Continental Army.
1776 Failed to secure French Canadian support; signed Declaration of Independence; sailed for France as one of three commissioners to negotiate alliance.
1777 Portrayed as popular hero in fur cap.
1778 Painted by Duplessis; modelled by Houdon; Franco-American treaty of alliance and commerce signed.

1779	Appointed sole minister plenipotentiary to French court.
1781	Appointed with others to join John Adams in negotiating peace with England.
1783	Signed peace treaty with England; reported details of French balloon ascents to Royal Society.
1784	Served on committee which discredited mesmerism; resumed writing autobiography.
1785	Returned to Philadelphia; elected president of Executive Council of Pennsylvania.
1787	Urged spirit of cooperation at Constitutional Convention; elected president of Pennsylvania Society for Promoting Abolition of Slavery.
1788	Began third part of autobiography; wrote will.
1789	Added codicil with bequests to Boston and Philadelphia.
1790	Died in Philadelphia, April 17.

Benjamin Franklin   *A Perspective*

Benjamin Franklin was born in Boston on January 17, 1706. His father Josiah, a tallow chandler and soapmaker, had come from England about 1682 with the mother of his first seven children. After her death he married Abiah Folger of Nantucket, who, wrote Franklin in his *Autobiography*, had "an excellent constitution: she suckled all her ten children."[1] Of these, Benjamin was the youngest son, with two younger sisters. He recalled as many as thirteen of the children sitting at one time at his parents' table, along with "some sensible friend or neighbor" with whom his father "always took care to start some ingenious or useful topic for discourse, which might tend to improve the minds of his children."

Benjamin's brothers were apprenticed to various trades; but, he wrote, "I was put to the grammar-school at eight years of age, my father intending to devote me, as the tithe of his sons, to the service of the Church." Although he had been reading since before he could remember, and learned very quickly in school, he stayed less than a year, for his father decided that neither could he afford to send his son on to college, nor could Benjamin subsist on "the mean living many so educated were afterwards able to obtain." He briefly attended a school for writing and arithmetic, and then remained at home to help with candlemaking.

He longed to go to sea. Fearing he would do just that, his father apprenticed him when he was twelve to his older brother James, a printer. Benjamin had for years read voraciously, not only the polemical religious treatises in his father's library, but Cotton Mather's *Essays to Do Good,* John Bunyan's *The Pilgrim's Progress* and other "works in separate little volumes," Plutarch's *Lives,* a collection of some forty short volumes of history, and any other books he could buy or borrow. Such a "bookish inclination" was thought to suit him for the printer's trade, and, indeed, he enjoyed his association with the booksellers' apprentices as it enabled him to borrow a wider variety of reading matter.

He became interested in writing himself, and composed a few ballads, the first of which, *The Lighthouse Tragedy,* was printed by James and sold very well. But his father told him his verse was trash. He thereupon set about developing a strong prose style, studying that of the authors he thought most eloquent, and inventing exercises in composition for himself.

In August, 1721, his brother James began to print a newspaper, *The New-England Courant.* At that time Boston was suffering a terrible smallpox epidemic, and Cotton Mather, together with the majority of the local clergy, urged the population to have themselves inoculated. This procedure, unlike the cowpox vaccination later developed by Jenner, brought on a mild case of smallpox, thereby preventing a person from contracting a more severe, often fatal case, through common contagion. On rare occasions an inoculated person died, and the frightened population suspected the clergy of promoting an evil plot. James Franklin, ever anti-clerical and dependent on popular support for the success of his paper, committed himself and the *Courant* to a violently anti-inoculation position.

When the inoculation controversy began to quiet down, James and those of his friends who contributed to the paper continued their satirical efforts in other directions. Benjamin longed to join their number. He slid his first effort, handwriting disguised and signed "Silence Dogood," under the door of the printing house. It met the standard of wit and style his brother and friends had set for their own pieces, and on April 2, 1722, it appeared on the front page of *The New-England Courant*.

Silence Dogood described herself as the widow of a country minister, with "a natural Inclination to observe and reprove the Faults of others."[2] In her fourth contribution to *The New-England Courant*, she recounted a dream in which she visited the Temple of Learning, to which parents sent their children, having "consulted their own Purses instead of their Children's Capacities" (NO. 1). Indeed, most of the children remained at the foot of Learning's throne "with Madam *Idleness* and her Maid *Ignorance*," until assisted by "those who had got up before them, and who, for the Reward perhaps of a *Pint of Milk*, or a *Piece of Plumb-Cake*, lent the Lubbers a helping Hand, and sat them in the Eye of the World, upon a Level with themselves." Silence Dogood's "Reverend Boarder" interpreted her dream: *"a lively Representation of* HARVARD COLLEGE."[3]

Benjamin did not get along well with James, who often lost his temper and beat him. "Perhaps," he concedes in his *Autobiography*, "I was too saucy and provoking." He was no doubt smug at the success of Silence Dogood, whose identity he had disclosed.

James, meanwhile, was printing comments which amused many of his readers while infuriating the Massachusetts government. He noted, for example, that the pirates harassing Boston trade would be pursued by the authorities "some time this month, wind and weather permitting." For this aspersion on their diligence, the humorless Council sent him to prison for several weeks.

Then, on January 14, 1723, James printed an essay on the hypocrites of New England, of whom Cotton Mather, though not named, was clearly the prime example. The Massachusetts Assembly was enraged, and forbade James to continue publication of the *Courant*. He thereupon arranged for Benjamin to assume the role of publisher. The younger brother's indenture paper was fully discharged and returned to him — for appearances' sake should the publication of the paper by an apprentice be questioned. Benjamin was obliged to sign a new, private indenture, but when he could stand James's tyrannical behavior no longer, he decided to leave the shop. James would not dare to make public the new indenture. But knowing what was on Benjamin's mind, he obtained from all his Boston colleagues a promise not to hire his youngest brother. Benjamin sold some of his books and in September sailed for New York and then Philadelphia, where he found employment with Keimer, an unskilled printer who badly needed a well-trained associate.

In April, 1724, he returned briefly to Boston to visit his family. He brought with him a letter to his father from Governor Keith of Pennsylvania, who urged the elder Franklin to set his son up with his own printing shop, which, he observed, would receive all the government's business. Josiah Franklin thought it ill advised to risk the capital required to outfit the business on behalf of a boy of eighteen. But he was pleased with the good reputation of his son. Benjamin wrote that his father bade him goodbye, "telling me, that by steady industry and a prudent parsimony I might save enough by the time I was one-and-twenty to set me up; and that, if I came near the matter, he would help me out with the rest."

When young Franklin returned to Philadelphia, Governor Keith offered to send him to England with letters of introduction and of credit so that he could purchase the necessary press, typefaces and other supplies to establish himself in business. After many delays the ship sailed for England. On Christmas Eve, 1724, Franklin arrived in London, where, as he related it, he discovered to his dismay that Governor Keith had reneged on his promise to send letters of credit with the captain. A fellow passenger, Mr. Denham, told him this was hardly surprising, "and he laught at the notion of the governor's giving me a letter of credit, having, as he said, no credit to give."

But Denham looked out for Franklin, and gave him the introductions necessary to find work. While employed at

Samuel Palmer's, Franklin set the type for Wollaston's *The Religion of Nature* (NO. 2) and, finding fault with the author's logic, he disputed it in a metaphysical essay entitled *A Dissertation on Liberty and Necessity, Pleasure and Pain*, which he printed himself. Palmer was impressed by his employee's astuteness and appalled by his philosophy. But other readers of the pamphlet were more favorably impressed by Franklin's ideas, sought him out, and introduced him to their friends among London's intelligentsia.

His reputation as a conversationalist was soon matched by his reknown as a swimming instructor. Since childhood he had "delighted with the exercise, had studied and practiced all Thévenot's motions and positions" (NOS. 3 and 4), had invented a rudimentary pair of swim fins, and had pulled himself through the water across a lake using a kite as a sail. He taught several of his friends to swim, and would have stayed in England to instruct the sons of Sir William Wyndham had not Denham urged him to return with him to Pennsylvania as assistant in his store.

They sailed for Philadelphia on July 23, 1726, and arrived October 11. The following spring both he and Denham contracted a terrible fever, of which Denham died. He left Franklin a small legacy. When Denham's executors took over the business, Franklin returned to Keimer's shop. Here he trained a number of newly indentured apprentices, cut the ornamental copperplates for paper money to be issued by New Jersey, and with Keimer spent three months in that Colony printing it. He made numerous friends among the officers of the province who supervised and tallied the printing of the bills, and corresponded with many of them afterwards. Shortly after his return from New Jersey, he and Hugh Meredith, a fellow printer, left Keimer's establishment and set up shop for themselves. Thanks to Franklin's craftsmanship, business thrived.

In 1727 Franklin organized ten friends into "a club of mutual improvement," which he called the Junto. Cotton Mather had proposed the formation of discussion groups in

NO. 4 All his life Franklin enjoyed swimming. As a child he studied Thévenot's *L'Art de Nager Demontré par Figures.* Engravings copied from that book illustrate *The Art of Swimming,* a compilation of instructions which includes "Cautions to Learners, and Advice to Bathers" gleaned from the writings of "the late Celebrated Dr. Benjamin Franklin."

THE
ART OF SWIMMING,

MADE

SAFE, EASY, PLEASANT,

AND

HEALTHFUL,

BY

ATTENTION TO THE INSTRUCTIONS

HEREIN SET FORTH,

AMONG WHICH ARE,

How to go into the water	Suspension by the chin
How to begin learning to swim	To tread water
How to return back swimming	How to change hand and foot
To float with your face upwards	To swim with your legs tied
How to turn in the water	To creep
The turn called ringing the bells	To sit in the water
Turning or rolling round	To cut your toe nails
To swim backwards	To show four parts of your body
To turn laying along	To swim holding up one leg
To make a circle	To swim holding up both hands
To turn in an upright posture	To boot yourself
To advance with your hands joined	The leap of the goat
To swim on your side	How to dive
To swim with both hands still	The perpendicular descent
To swim with one leg in the opposite hand	To swim under water
	How to rise after diving
To swim like a dog	To make a circle under water
To beat water	The agility of the dolphin
To keep one foot above the water	How to fly a kite in the water.
To show both feet	

TO WHICH ARE ADDED,

CAUTIONS TO LEARNERS,

AND

ADVICE TO BATHERS,

BY THE LATE CELEBRATED

DR. BENJAMIN FRANKLIN.

LONDON:
PRINTED AND PUBLISHED BY J. FAIRBURN, 110, MINORIES.

Price Sixpence.

his *Essays to Do Good.* The inoculation controversy notwithstanding, Franklin had continued to be impressed by the philosophy in these *Essays* which he had read as a boy. His association of thoughtful, congenial men who met to exchange ideas, to speculate on the causes of curious phenomena, and to discuss solutions to mutual problems grew from the idea planted by Cotton Mather.

In April, 1729, Franklin wrote and printed anonymously *The Nature and Necessity of a Paper Currency,* and when the Pennsylvania Assembly voted an issue of £30,000 paper money, Franklin benefited from the expanded economy it encouraged. In 1731 he reaped more direct benefits from his stand on monetary policies when he received the commission to print a newly authorized issue of £40,000.

When Keimer's business began to fail in September, 1729, Franklin bought out a newspaper Keimer had recently started, shortened its title to *The Pennsylvania Gazette,* and greatly improved its quality and increased its circulation. He further diversified his business with a stationery shop that sold not only writing materials but legal forms and books. In January, 1730, he and Meredith were appointed printers to the Pennsylvania Assembly. As he recalled in his *Autobiography,* he "went on swimmingly."

The parents of the young women he found attractive, however, were not impressed by the prospects of a man in the printing trade, and would not provide a dowry for the daughters he courted. So he renewed his friendship with Deborah Read. He had lodged with her parents while employed by Keimer, and before he sailed for London in 1724 they had become engaged. During his long, uncommunicative absence, she had married a potter, who had deserted her and was thought — but not known — to be dead. Franklin "took her to wife, September 1st, 1730."

About this time Franklin suggested to the members of the Junto that they pool their books to form a reference library for their meeting room. This arrangement was not entirely satisfactory, so the following year he proposed a library to be supported by the annual subscriptions of fifty members. Books were imported from England and lent to the subscribers. The scheme worked, and after several years the Library Company was incorporated under a permanent charter. The idea, too, flourished, and subscription libraries were established in many Colonial towns.

Franklin published the first number of his *Almanack* in 1732, under the name of "Richard Saunders." This booklet of monthly calendars, with long range weather forecasts, tide tables, and both astronomical and astrological information, was enlivened with witty observations and proverbs. Franklin wrote some himself; others he rewrote, adapted, or quoted. They "contained the wisdom of many ages and nations" — and, in most cases, Franklin had found them to be true from "Experience [who] keeps a dear school":

>THE PROUD HATE PRIDE — IN OTHERS.
>
>THREE MAY KEEP A SECRET,
>IF TWO OF THEM ARE DEAD.
>
>'TIS MORE NOBLE TO FORGIVE, AND MORE MANLY
>TO DESPISE, THAN TO REVENGE AN INJURY.
>
>WRITE WITH THE LEARNED,
>PRONOUNCE WITH THE VULGAR.
>
>'TIS AGAINST SOME MEN'S PRINCIPLE
>TO PAY INTEREST, AND SEEMS AGAINST OTHERS'
>INTEREST TO PAY THE PRINCIPAL.
>
>KEEP YOUR EYES WIDE OPEN BEFORE MARRIAGE,
>HALF SHUT AFTERWARDS.
>
>YOU CAN BEAR YOUR OWN FAULTS,
>AND WHY NOT A FAULT IN YOUR WIFE.

The almanac for 1748 went on sale in September, 1747, as *Poor Richard Improved: Being an Almanack and Ephemeris of the Motions of the Sun and Moon . . . Together with Useful Tables, Chronological Observations, and Entertaining Remarks . . . By Richard Saunders, Philom[ath]. Philadelphia: Printed and Sold by B. Franklin* (NO. 5). The "improvement" was the expansion from twenty-four to thirty-six pages, which allowed room for more of the "entertaining Remarks" and instructive essays.

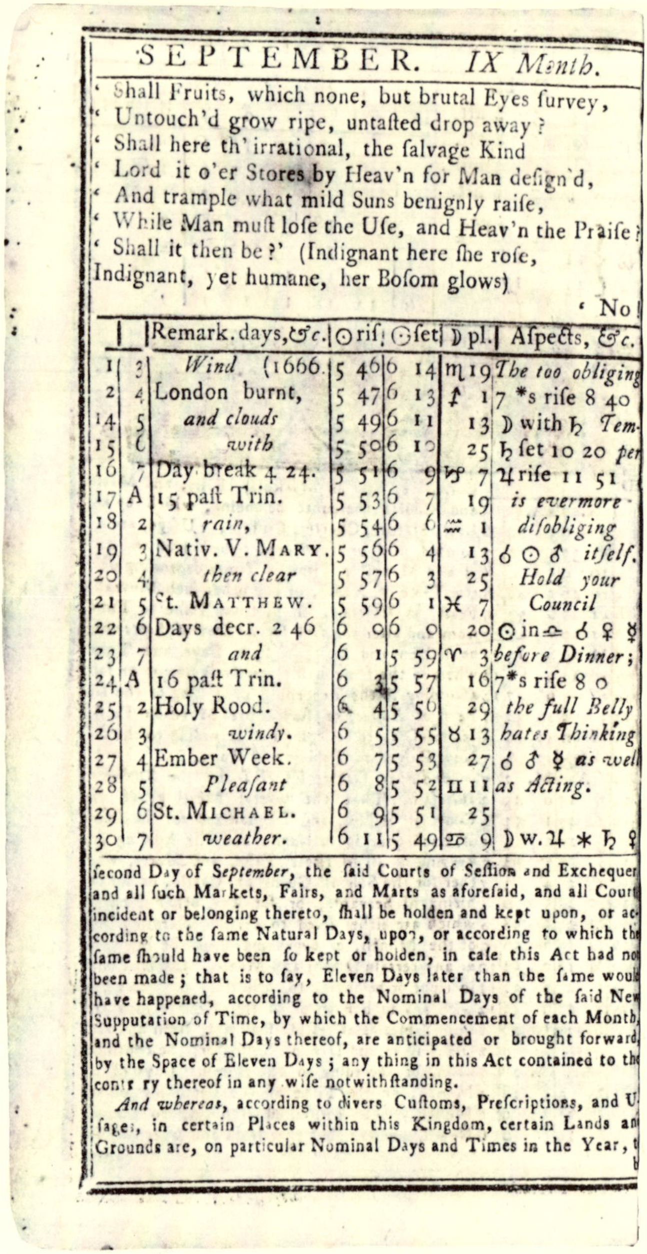

SEPTEMBER. *IX Month.*

'Shall Fruits, which none, but brutal Eyes ſurvey,
'Untouch'd grow ripe, untaſted drop away?
'Shall here th' irrational, the ſalvage Kind
'Lord it o'er Stores by Heav'n for Man deſign'd,
'And trample what mild Suns benignly raiſe,
'While Man muſt loſe the Uſe, and Heav'n the Praiſe?
'Shall it then be?' (Indignant here ſhe roſe,
Indignant, yet humane, her Boſom glows)
'No!

		Remark. days, &c.	☉ riſ.	☉ ſet	☽ pl.	Aſpects, &c.
1	3	*Wind* (1666.	5 46	6 14	♏ 19	*The too obliging*
2	4	London burnt,	5 47	6 13	♐ 1	7 *s riſe 8 40
14	5	*and clouds*	5 49	6 11	13	☽ with ♄ *Tem-*
15	6	*with*	5 50	6 10	25	♄ ſet 10 20 *per*
16	7	Day break 4 24.	5 51	6 9	♑ 7	♃ riſe 11 51
17	A	15 paſt Trin.	5 53	6 7	19	*is evermore*
18	2	*rain,*	5 54	6 6	♒ 1	*diſobliging*
19	3	Nativ. V. Mary.	5 56	6 4	13	☌ ☉ ♂ *itſelf.*
20	4	*then clear*	5 57	6 3	25	*Hold your*
21	5	St. Matthew.	5 59	6 1	♓ 7	*Council*
22	6	Days decr. 2 46	6 0	6 0	20	☉ in ♎ ☌ ♀ ☿
23	7	*and*	6 1	5 59	♈ 3	*before Dinner;*
24	A	16 paſt Trin.	6 3	5 57	16	7*s riſe 8 0
25	2	Holy Rood.	6 4	5 56	29	*the full Belly*
26	3	*windy.*	6 5	5 55	♉ 13	*hates Thinking*
27	4	Ember Week.	6 7	5 53	27	☌ ♂ ☿ *as well*
28	5	*Pleaſant*	6 8	5 52	♊ 11	*as Acting.*
29	6	St. Michael.	6 9	5 51	25	
30	7	*weather.*	6 11	5 49	♋ 9	☽ w. ♃ ✱ ♄ ♀

ſecond Day of *September*, the ſaid Courts of Seſſion and Exchequer and all ſuch Markets, Fairs, and Marts as aforeſaid, and all Court incident or belonging thereto, ſhall be holden and kept upon, or according to the ſame Natural Days, upon, or according to which th ſame ſhould have been ſo kept or holden, in caſe this Act had no been made; that is to ſay, Eleven Days later than the ſame woul have happened, according to the Nominal Days of the ſaid New Supputation of Time, by which the Commencement of each Month and the Nominal Days thereof, are anticipated or brought forward by the Space of Eleven Days; any thing in this Act contained to th contrary thereof in any wiſe notwithſtanding.

And whereas, according to divers Cuſtoms, Preſcriptions, and Uſages, in certain Places within this Kingdom, certain Lands an Grounds are, on particular Nominal Days and Times in the Year, t

NO. 6 "SEPTEMBER hath XIX Days" in 1752, when English-speaking countries adopted the Gregorian (New Style) calendar. September 3

September hath xix Days.

D. H.			Planets Places.						
First Q.	15	8 mor.	D.	☉	♄	♃	♂	♀	☿	☽s L.
Full ●	23	8 mor.		♍	♎	♋	♍	♏	♎	
Last Q.	30	10 mor.	1	20	19	12	23	27	12	N. 0
☊ { 1 ♏ 17 Deg.			17	25	19	12	26	♎ 3	11	4
22	16		22	♎ 0	19	13	29	9	8	4
			27	5	19	13	♎ 3	16	2	S. 1

D.	☽ set	☽ sou. T.	Old Stile	
1	8 54	3 51	6	be opened for Common of Pasture, and other
2	9 37	4 39	7	Purposes; and at other Times, the Owners
14	10 24	5 27	8 3	and Occupiers of such Lands and Grounds have
15	11 17	6 17	9 4	a Right to inclose or shut up the same, for their
16	12 9	7 6	10 5	own private Use; and there is in many other
17	M. 9	7 53	10 6	Instances, a temporary and distinct Property
18	1 5	8 41	11 7	and Right vested in different Persons, in and to
19	2 5	9 25	12 8	many such Lands and Grounds, according to
20	3 0	10 9	1 9	certain Nominal Days and Times in the Year:
21	4 0	10 55	1 10	*And whereas,* the anticipating or bringing for-
22	Moon	11 41	2 11	ward the said Nominal Days and Times, by
23	rises.	12 28	3 12	the Space of eleven Days, according to the
24	A	M. 28	3 13	said New Method of Supputation, might be at-
25	7 4	1 16	4 14	tended with many Inconveniencies; *Be it there-*
26	7 44	2 12	5 15	*fore further Declared, Provided, and Enacted,*
27	8 29	3 7	6 16	by the Authority aforesaid, That nothing in
28	9 25	4 5	7 17	this Act contained, shall extend, or be con-
29	10 25.5	3	8 18	strued to extend, to accelerate or anticipate the
30	11 30	6 0	9 19	Days or Times for the opening, inclosing, or

shutting up any such Lands or Grounds as afore-
said, or the Days or Times on which any such temporary or distinct
Property or Right in or to any such Lands or Grounds as aforesaid is
to commence; but that all such Lands and Grounds as aforesaid,
shall, from and after the said second Day of *September,* be, from
Time to Time respectively opened, inclosed, or shut up, and such
temporary and distinct Property and Right in and to such Lands and
Grounds as aforesaid, shall commence and begin upon the same
natural Days and Times on which the same should have been so respectively opened, inclosed, or shut up, or would have commenced
or

*For the Convenience of our Readers who may frequently have Occa-
sion to know what Day of the Calendar according to the New Stile, cor-
responds to any particular Day of the Calendar according to the Old Stile,
we shall henceforth in the last Column of this Right-hand Page put
down the Days according to the said Old Stile Calendar.*

through 13 were omitted, permitting the restoration of September 22 as the date of the autumnal equinox.

The 1757 *Almanack* included a preface in the form of "the harangue of a wise old man to the people attending an auction," a device which was used to string together a synthesis of the admonitions to be industrious and frugal he had so often heard and practiced during his boyhood. Under the titles *The Way to Wealth* and *Father Abraham's Speech*, it was widely reprinted in newspapers and on sheets "to be stuck up in houses," both in Britain and on the Continent, where it was translated into French (NOS. 8 and 9).

Richard Saunders was not merely Franklin's pseudonym; he became Benjamin Franklin's mentor. Following his own advice, the printer prospered. In his *Autobiography,* he recalled: "my business was now continually augmenting, and my circumstances growing daily easier, my newspaper having become very profitable." *The Pennsylvania Gazette* was also the vehicle through which he introduced the people of Philadelphia to his suggestions for municipal improvements. "I considered my newspaper, also, as another means of communicating instruction . . . and sometimes published little pieces of my own, which had been first composed for reading in our Junto."

One of these pieces was "on the different accidents and carelessness by which houses were set on fire, with cautions against them." In 1736 it "gave rise to a project": the bucket brigade called the Union Fire Company, first of the many small volunteer fire departments organized in Philadelphia. Another paper read in the Junto led to the reorganization of the city watch into an effective constabulary. Unable to improve Philadelphia weather, he instead invented the Pennsylvania Fireplace, now known as the Franklin Stove, "for the better warming of rooms, and at the same time saving fuel."

In 1744, he circulated plans for the organization of an American Philosophical Society, modelled on the Royal Society of London. It was to be an association of scientists in the Colonies, with its administrative center at Philadelphia. That same year he designed and printed his friend

LA SCIENCE

DU BONHOMME RICHARD,

O U

MOYEN FACILE

DE PAYER LES IMPÔTS.

TRADUIT DE L'ANGLOIS.

A PHILADELPHIE.
Et se trouve
A PARIS, chez RUAULT, Libraire
rue de la Harpe.

1777.

NO. 9 "Poor Richard" was also famous in France.

(iv)

however, (among whom I had the Honour to be ranked) obtained Copies of it in M. S. And, as I believed it to be in itself equal at least, if not far preferable to any other Translation of the same Piece extant in our Language, besides the Advantage it has of so many valuable Notes, which at the same time they clear up the Text, are highly instructive and entertaining; I resolved to give it an Impression, being confident that the Publick would not unfavourably receive it.

A certain Freed-man of *Cicero*'s is reported to have said of a medicinal Well, discovered in his Time, wonderful for the Virtue of its Waters in restoring Sight to the Aged, *That it was a Gift of the bounti-*

NO. 10 For the myopic, Franklin set in large type James Logan's

bountiful Gods to *Men*, *to the end that all might now have the Pleasure of reading his Master's Works.* As that Well, if still in being, is at too great a Distance for our Use, I have, *Gentle Reader,* as thou seest, printed this Piece of *Cicero*'s in a large and fair Character, that those who begin to think on the Subject of OLD-AGE, (which seldom happens till their Sight is somewhat impair'd by its Approaches) may not, in Reading, by the *Pain* small Letters give the Eyes, feel the *Pleasure* of the Mind in the least allayed.

I shall add to these few Lines my hearty Wish, that this first Translation of a *Classic* in this *Western World*, may be followed with many others, performed with equal

James Logan's translation of Cicero's *Cato Major, or His Discourse of Old-Age*, for which he supplied a preface explaining and extolling his choice of a large, legible type (NO. 10).

A portrait painted about this time by Robert Feke apparently shows Franklin as a prosperous businessman and respected civil servant (NO. 11). But does it depict *Benjamin Franklin*? There is speculation that it represents his brother John, of Newport and Boston. The confusion arises from the fact that at the time of John's death in 1756 portraits of both John and Benjamin passed to John's heirs, and one is now lost. It is strange, too, that Benjamin Franklin, who committed so much to pen and ink, left no mention of the circumstances under which this likeness was painted. Was it done in Boston or Newport in 1743 or 1746, or in Philadelphia in 1746 or 1749? Artist and subject were both in these cities at each of these times. After exhaustive research on the matter, Charles Sellers has concluded that the painting does indeed portray Benjamin Franklin, and R. Peter Mooz further concludes that the manner of painting points to the year 1746.[4]

The artist provided as little information on the portrait as did his subject, and his identity, too, is uncertain. A Robert Feke born in Oyster Bay, New York, about 1707 is probably the Robert Feke who married in Newport, Rhode Island, in 1742, and who signed and dated several portraits in the 1740s. The earliest of these is the handsome group *Isaac Royall and His Family*, inscribed on the back with the names of the sitters and "Finisht Sept. 15th, 1741/by Robert Feke." This painting now hangs at the Harvard Law School in Langdell Hall. Franklin's likeness, which has been attributed also to John Greenwood and Joseph Badger, is not signed. But the strong stylistic affinity to such signed portraits as that of Tench Francis (Philadelphia, 1746) and the more accomplished suite of four paintings portraying William and James Bowdoin and their wives, all signed and dated 1748, has resulted in the present scholarly consensus that the artist was indeed Robert Feke.

While the arts and commerce were flourishing in the Colonies, England was at war with Spain and France. By the summer of 1747 the raids of Spanish and French privateers along the Delaware River had become so audacious that Philadelphia was threatened. While tactfully maneuvering to retain his prestige among the Quakers, Franklin wrote, and on November 17 published, an anonymous pamphlet, *Plain Truth*. This appeal for a voluntary association for defense was followed a few days later by a specific plan of action. Franklin set about recruiting and equipping an organization of volunteers. He organized a lottery so that funds would be available to the city to buy a battery of cannon. In his printing shop he sold muskets and ammunition belts.

Peace came in the spring of 1749 and Franklin returned to a project he had first considered six years earlier: founding an academy. As he later wrote in the *Autobiography*, "the first step I took was to associate in the design a number of active friends, of whom the Junto furnished a good part; the next was to write and publish a pamphlet entitled *Proposals Relating to the Education of Youth in Pensilvania*" (NO. 12). Within a few weeks a subscription was raised and twenty-four trustees elected; then a house was rented, schoolmasters hired, documents signed, and the Academy of Philadelphia — now the University of Pennsylvania — was opened on January 7, 1751.

Meanwhile, Franklin had been continuing his own education. He taught himself French, then Italian and Spanish. He "was surprised to find, on looking over a Latin Testament, that [he] understood so much more of that language than [he] imagined," that he resumed its study some twenty years after his brief introduction at the grammar school.

Hardly was the academy in session, before Franklin was recruiting his friends to assist in promoting a hospital for the sick of Philadelphia. He solicited the financial aid of the Assembly through yet another small book, *Some Account of the Pennsylvania Hospital*, and in 1755 he composed the inscription for the cornerstone.

NO. 11 Portrait of Benjamin Franklin, by Robert Feke, ca. 1746. Oil on canvas. H. 127.5 x 102.5 cm.

The earliest known portrait of Franklin shows him as a respected printer and civic leader. In 1747 he turned over the management of his printing business to a partner, in order to devote more time to his experiments with electricity. He recorded the results of this research in letters to Peter Collinson, which he had copied for James Bowdoin in October 1750.

Portrait of James Bowdoin II (1726-1790), by Robert Feke. Signed and dated, l.l.: R F Pinx/1748. Oil on canvas. H. 127 x 102 cm. Courtesy of Bowdoin College; bequest of Mrs. Sarah Bowdoin Dearborn. Bowdoin, a young Boston merchant, met Franklin in Philadelphia in 1750, beginning a friendship that continued until their deaths a few months apart forty years later. Franklin included some of Bowdoin's letters in late editions of *Experiments and Observations* (see p. 71).

(10)

That the boarding Scholars diet ‡ together, plainly, temperately, and frugally.

That to keep them in Health, and to ſtrengthen and render active their Bodies, they be frequently * exercis'd in Running, Leaping, Wreſtling, and Swimming †, &c.

That

‡ Perhaps it would be beſt if none of the Scholars were to diet abroad. *Milton* is of that Opinion *(Tractate of Education)* for that much Time would elſe be loſt, and many ill Habits got.

* *Milton* propoſes, that an Hour and Half before Dinner ſhould be allow'd for Exerciſe, and recommends among other Exerciſes, the handling of Arms, but perhaps this may not be thought neceſſary here. *Turnbull*, p. 318. ſays, " Corporal Exerciſe invigorates the Soul as well as the Body ; let one be kept cloſely to Reading, without allowing him any Reſpite from Thinking, or any Exerciſe to his Body, and were it poſſible to preſerve long, by ſuch a Method, his Liking to Study and Knowledge, yet we ſhould ſoon find ſuch an one become no leſs ſoft in his Mind than in his outward Man. Both Mind and Body would thus become gradually too relaxed, too much unbraced for the Fatigues and Duties of active Life. Such is the Union between Soul and Body, that the ſame Exerciſes which are conducive, when rightly managed, to conſolidate or ſtrengthen the former, are likewiſe equally neceſſary and fit to produce Courage, Firmneſs, and manly Vigour, in the latter. For this, and other Reaſons, certain hardy Exerciſes were reckoned by the Antients an eſſential Part in the Formation of a liberal Character ; and ought to have their Place in Schools where Youth are taught the Languages and Sciences." See p. 318 to 323.

† 'Tis ſuppos'd that every Parent would be glad to have their Children ſkill'd in *Swimming*, if it might be learnt in a Place choſen for its Safety, and under the Eye of a careful Perſon. Mr. *Locke* ſays, p. 9. in his *Treatiſe of Education* ; " 'Tis that ſaves many a Man's Life ; and the *Romans* thought it ſo neceſſary, that they rank'd it with Letters ; and it was the common Phraſe to mark one ill educated, and good for nothing, that he had neither learnt to read nor to ſwim ; *Nec Literas didicit nec Natare*. But beſides the gaining a Skill which may ſerve him at Need, the Advantages to Health by often Bathing

(11)

That they have peculiar Habits to diftinguifh them from other Youth, if the Academy be in or near the Town; for this, among other Reafons, that their Behaviour may be the better obferved.

As to their STUDIES, it would be well if they could be taught *every Thing* that is ufeful, and *every Thing* that is ornamental: But Art is long, and their Time is fhort. It is therefore propos'd that they learn thofe Things that are likely to be *moft ufeful* and *moft ornamental*. Regard being had to the feveral Profeffions for which they are intended.

All fhould be taught to write a *fair Hand*, and fwift, as that is ufeful to All. And with

B 2 it

ing in cold Water during the Heat of the Summer, are fo many, that I think nothing need be faid to encourage it."

'Tis fome Advantage befides, to be free from the flavifh Terrors many of thofe feel who cannot fwim, when they are oblig'd to be on the Water even in croffing a Ferry.

Mr. *Hutchinfon*, in his *Dialogues concerning Education*, 2 Vols. Octavo, lately publifh'd, fays, Vol. 2. p. 297. " I would have the Youth accuftomed to fuch Exercifes as will harden their Conftitution, as Riding, Running, Swimming, Shooting, and the like."

Charlemagne, Founder of the *German* Empire, brought up his Sons hardily, and even his Daughters were inur'd to Induftry. *Henry* the Great of *France*, faith Monf. *Rhodex*, " was not permitted by his Grand-father to be brought up with Delicacy, who well knew that *feldom lodgeth other than a mean and feeble Spirit in an effeminate and tender Body*. He commanded that the Boy fhould be accuftomed to run, to leap, to climb the Rocks and Mountains; that by fuch Means he might be inured to Labour, &c. His ordinary Food alfo was of coarfe Bread, Beef, Cheefe and Garlick; his Cloathing plain and coarfe, and often he went barefoot and bareheaded." *Walker of Education*, p. 17, 18.

In 1759 he began distribution of a pamphlet which urged the public to protect itself from smallpox through inoculation. Although in 1721 *The New-England Courant* had ridiculed Cotton Mather for promoting inoculation, Franklin later realized what a boon the practice was in preventing the spread of the disease. His little boy had died of smallpox in 1736, and Franklin, who never forgave himself for delaying the child's inoculation, published in *The Pennsylvania Gazette* a notice that his son had died not from the procedure, but because of its omission. Over the years he collected convincing statistics in support of inoculation, and these, together with Dr. William Heberden's instructions for inoculating, were the substance of his pamphlet.

Since the founding of the Junto and the Library Company, Franklin had had access to the writings of Europe's most distinguished scientists, with whose theories he familiarized himself. While in Boston in 1743 he saw electrical experiments performed by Dr. Archibald Spencer. The following year he sponsored Spencer's lectures in Philadelphia, and later bought some of his scientific apparatus. In 1745 the Library Company received from their generous patron, Peter Collinson, a Quaker merchant and Fellow of the Royal Society of London, a "glass tube" with instructions for its use in performing experiments with electricity. On March 28, 1747, Franklin wrote to Collinson that he and his coexperimenters had "observed some particular phænomena that we look upon to be new," and that "for my own part, I never before engaged in any study that so totally engrossed my attention and my time as this has lately done."[5]

Franklin was free to be so engrossed because in 1744 another London correspondent, the printer William Strahan, had recommended to his care a Scottish associate named David Hall, in hopes that the young man might set up his own business. He worked as Franklin's foreman until the summer of 1747, when Franklin made him managing partner — and turned his own attention to discovering the nature of electricity.

In a steady stream of letters to Collinson, Franklin related the outcome of his many experiments, and stated the new hypotheses he proposed to test. Progress was often discouragingly slow, and on August 14, 1747, he wrote his friend: "In going on with these Experiments, how many pretty Systems do we build, which we soon find ourselves oblig'd to destroy! If there is no other Use discovered of Electricity, this, however, is something considerable, that it may *help to make a vain Man humble.*"[6] But other letters brought Collinson news of the discovery of several principles governing the behavior of "electrical fire": the law of conservation of charge, and a theory explaining the mechanism of induced electrostatic charges; also, the manner in which these phenomena account for the operation of a condenser such as the Leyden jar.

Franklin's observations of electricity led him to the conclusion that the lightning discharge is an electrical phenomenon. He listed twelve properties common to lightning and electricity. He then proposed an experiment deriving from his research with pointed rods and with grounding to determine whether lightning, like electricity, "is attracted by points." Details of this proposed experiment, which required that a man stand on an insulating stool inside a sentry box equipped with a sharply pointed thirty-foot rod, the box to be fixed atop a high tower or steeple, were also sent to Peter Collinson.

In 1751 Collinson collected the letters on electricity that Franklin had sent to him and to others, and published them as a little book entitled *Experiments and Observations on Electricity, Made at Philadelphia in America, by Mr. Benjamin Franklin* (NO. 13). Dr. John Fothergill, influential Quaker physician and botanist (NO. 68), edited the text and wrote the preface. Thomas-François Dalibard, at the suggestion of the eminent naturalist Buffon, translated the book into French; he and his colleague Delor reported to the Paris Academy of Science in May, 1752, that they had each successfully carried out the proposed sentry box experiment. Then, in June, 1752, before news of the French successes had reached Philadelphia, Franklin — lacking high tower or steeple — devised another version of the experiment.

Franklin put illustrations such as this sentry box in the margins of his letters. Thomas Jeffries engraved them for a gatefold plate that was inserted in the published *Experiments and Observations*.

He constructed a silk kite with a pointed wire protruding a foot out of the top. To the end of the kite string he tied a ribbon, with a key at the knot. During a thunderstorm, the pointed wire drew the lightning to the wet kite and string, which conducted it to the key. Franklin, carefully holding only the dry silk ribbon, himself remained under cover and dry as he observed the electricity "stream out plentifully" from the key.[7]

The practical consequence of these experiments was the lightning rod. In the *Almanack* for the year 1753, Poor Richard wrote: "It has pleased God in his Goodness to Mankind, at length to discover to them the Means of securing their Habitations and other Buildings from Mischief by Thunder and Lightning." Then follow detailed instructions for affixing lightning rods to houses, barns, and ships.[8]

Among the many correspondents to whom Franklin communicated news of his experiments was James Bowdoin, who had visited him in Philadelphia in 1750. This able young man graduated from Harvard at the age of eighteen in 1745, and two years later inherited a share of the fortune his father had amassed in the shipping business. Young Bowdoin continued the family enterprises, but his real avocation was natural philosophy, as experimental science was then called. Franklin was impressed by his keen, inquisitive mind, and in October, 1750, sent him a copy of his collected letters on electricity with a request for his comments on them. The following autumn he again wrote Bowdoin to introduce his colleague Ebenezer Kinnersley (1711-1778), who was coming to Boston to give a series of lectures and demonstrations on electricity. Bowdoin wrote back on December 21 to say that Kinnersley's "experiments" had "been greatly pleasing to all sorts of people." He then offered lengthy comments not only on Kinnersley's demonstrations, but on some of the hypotheses in Franklin's letters which he thought to be shaky. He closed with a request for Franklin's writings on magnetism,[9] which he received by return mail.

On February 28, 1753, the subject of the correspondence shifted from electricity to astronomy. Franklin forwarded to Bowdoin a leaflet of instructions for making calculations relative to the transit of Mercury across the face of the sun, which was to take place on May 6. He asked Bowdoin "to promote the Making these Observations in New England."[10] Bowdoin replied that "a gentleman here, who is provided with the proper instruments, and well skilled in astronomy, intends to make the necessary observations."[11] This gentleman was undoubtedly John Winthrop, who had been Hollis Professor of Mathematics and Natural Philosophy at Harvard since Bowdoin's undergraduate years there, and whose observations of the transit of Mercury in 1740 had been published by the Royal Society (NOS. 14 and 15).

That Bowdoin was in close communication with the professors at Harvard is suggested by the letter Franklin wrote him on April 12, 1753, which begins: "I have shipt 18 Glass [Leyden] Jarrs in Casks well pack'd, on board Capt. Branscombe for Boston. 6 of them are for you, the rest I understand are for the College"[12] (NO. 16). Apparently it was not only Bowdoin, but his colleagues at Harvard as well, who were receiving scientific information and equipment from Franklin. Certainly, the faculty were aware of the esteem in which

NO. 14 John Singleton Copley painted this portrait of Professor John Winthrop, a keen observer of celestial and terrestrial phenomena. Winthrop's studies of the mass and density of comets was an original contribution to astronomy, while his realization that earthquakes are earth "waves" initiated the science of seismology. His precise calculations and meticulous observations of eclipses and transits were of great value to his fellow astronomers in England.

NO. 15 James Short made this portable reflecting telescope in London about 1740. It is the one seen in Copley's portrait of Winthrop.

Franklin was held in Europe following the publication there of *Experiments and Observations,* for on July 23, 1753, President Edward Holyoke (NO. 17) and the Fellows of Harvard

> Voted, That Whereas Mr. Benja. Franklyn of Philadelphia, hath made great Improvements in Philosophic Learning, & particularly wth. Respect to Electricity, Whereby his Repute hath been greatly advanc'd in the learned World, not only in Great-Britain, but ev'n in the Kingdom of France also, We therefore willing to do Honour to a Person of such considerable Improvements in Learning, Do admit him to the Degree of Master of Arts in Harvard-College. And it is hereby also directed, that the Diploma to be given, in this Regard, to the sd. Mr. Franklyn, be varied from the Common Form, aggreable to the Preamble of this Vote: And that this Vote to be presented to the Honble. & Revd. the Overseers for their Approbation.[13]

One of the Overseers was an amateur scientist, poet and notorious punster — the Reverend Mather Byles. He had been acquainted with Franklin during his boyhood in Boston, and apparently he was the member of the Governing Boards who proposed that Harvard honor the famous scientist. When many years later, on May 14, 1787, he wrote to Franklin to thank him for recommending him for a degree from the University of Aberdeen, Franklin replied that "it was in me only paying a Debt; for I remember with Gratitude, that I owe one of my first Academical Honours to your Recommendation."[14] It is probable that Bowdoin, too, urged the College to give Franklin special recognition.

Franklin's Master of Arts is often considered to be the first honorary degree granted by Harvard: that is, the first degree awarded not for academic achievement within the College, but for honorable accomplishments and contributions to man's store of knowledge made outside the academic circle — a degree conferred on a recipient who reflected distinction back on the College (NO. 18).

Franklin was honored twice again during the year. From

NO. 17 Edward Holyoke was an able amateur scientist who, during his thirty-two years as President of Harvard College, encouraged Professor Winthrop's research, expeditions, and teaching. Copley has portrayed him sitting in the chair still used by Harvard presidents on ceremonial occasions.

NO. 18 (overleaf) Master of Arts diploma, signed by President Holyoke and the Fellows of Harvard College, which was presented to Benjamin Franklin.

Senatus Academiæ

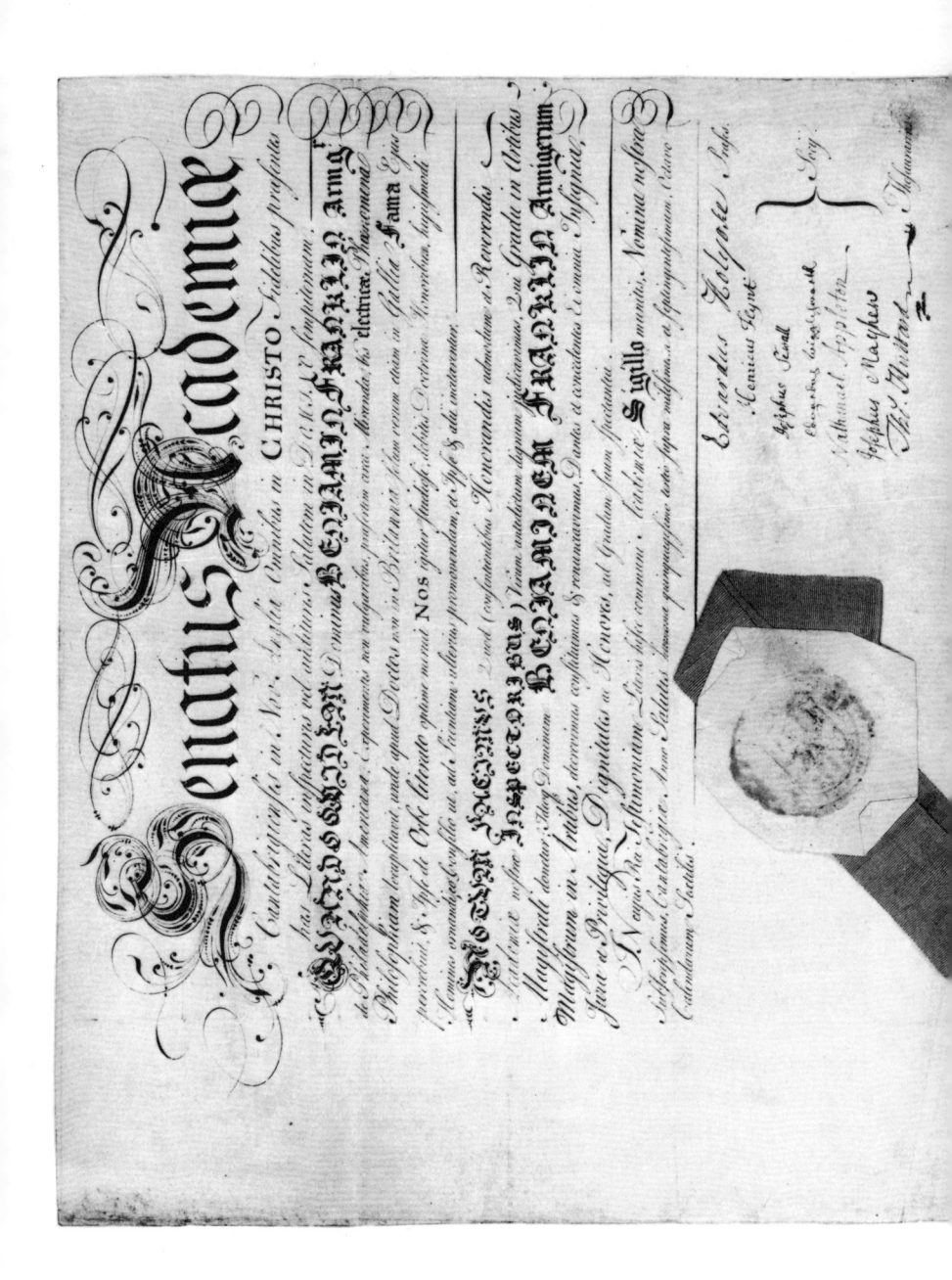

Cantabrigiensis in Nov. Anglia Omnibus in CHRISTO Fidelibus presentes has Literas inspecturis vel audituris, Salutem in Domino sempiternam.

QUANDOQUIDEM Dominus BENJAMIN FRANKLIN Armiger de Philadelphia, Americanus, experimentis non vulgaribus, profectum artis Monadis his electricæ Phænomena Philosophicam templarit, unde apud Doctos non in Britannia solum rerum etiam in Gallia Fama Ejus provenit, & Ipse ob Orbi literato quam merui Nos igitur studiis debita Doctorum Nomerchan, hujusmodi Meritas comendafti oportia ex, aut Suidam ulterius promovendam, ei Ipse & alii cohortentur.

NOVERINT IGITUR Quod (consentientibus Honerandis admodum ac Reverendis Academiæ nostræ INSPECTORIBUS) Virum antedictum dignum judicaverimus, Dei Gratia in Artibus Magistrali donatus; Atque Dominum BENJAMIN FRANKLIN Armigerum Magistrum in Artibus, decrevimus constituimus & renuntiavimus, Damus et concedimus Ei omnia Insignia Jura et Privilegia, Dignitates ac Honores, ad Gradum suum spectantia.

In Noviora Testimonium, Sacris hisce communi Academiæ Sigillo munitis, Nomina nostra Subscripsimus Cantabrigiæ, Anno Salutis humanæ quinquagesimo octavo supra millesimo, et septingentesimo, Octavo Calendarum Sextilis.

Edvardus Holyoke, *Præfes*
Henricus Flynt

Josephus Sewall
Ebenezer Wigglesworth
Nathanael Appleton
Josephus Mayhew
B. Prescott

Yale, where he was also in communication with fellow scientists, he received a second Master of Arts degree. Then the Royal Society awarded him its highest honor, the Copley Medal. Three years later he was elected a Fellow of the Society.

Franklin, who as Silence Dogood had so scathingly derided Harvard students three decades earlier, now added the College to the growing list of institutions he wished to help with fund-raising schemes. On September 11, 1755, he wrote to Thomas Hancock concerning "the Inconvenience attending the Want of a Fund to increase and improve your College Library."[15] He proposed that Hancock, being "a Friend to the College," solicit subscriptions to such a fund among his acquaintances. He enclosed a subscription form on which he pledged "Four Pistoles" annually for five years, with space below for the signatures of subsequent subscribers. He also enclosed an order to his brother John Franklin, postmaster of Boston, to pay the first installment (NO. 19).

Since no further subscribers signed, and since Franklin's money order was not negotiated, one may assume that Thomas Hancock did not pursue Franklin's suggestion. But Hancock was, indeed, a "Friend to the College." He gave books and "philosophical apparatus" including the reflecting telescope with which Professor Winthrop observed the transit of Venus in 1763, and through his will he established the Hancock Professorship of Hebrew and Other Oriental Languages — the first chair in the Colonies to be endowed by an American.

As the war between England and France over the frontiers of their North American colonies worsened, Franklin became increasingly involved in political affairs. In the spring of 1754 the British ordered the Colonial governors to meet at Albany to adopt a consistent policy toward the Indians, nearly all of whom were allying themselves with the French. Franklin attended, and proposed what came to be known as the Albany Plan of Union. Although it was adopted by the Albany Congress, it was rejected by every Colony.

Sir— Philadelphia 11th Sept. 1753.

You may remember that when I last had the Pleasure of seeing you, I mention'd the Inconvenience attending the Want of a Fund to increase and improve your College Library.

I imagined that a Subscription set on foot for that purpose might with proper Management produce something considerable. I know you are a Friend to the College, and therefore take the Freedom of inclosing a Paper of that kind, and recommending it to your Care, to procure (if you approve of the design) a suitable Number of Hands to it. Five and twenty Subscribers at 4 Pistoles Each p. Annum would in five Years produce 500 Pistoles, which if all laid out in Books would make a handsome Addition to the Library, or if put to Interest, would produce a little Annual Income sufficient to procure the best new Books published in each Year. Some might perhaps Subscribe more than four Pistoles p. Annum and others less; and I think that a single Pistole or half a Pistole should not be refused; Tho' such small Sums might occasion a little more Trouble in Receiving or Collecting.

I send withal an Order on my Brother, for my first Year's Payment. 'Tis but a Trifle compar'd with my hearty Good will and Respect to the College; but a small Seed properly Sown, sometimes produces a large and fruitful Tree; which I sincerely wish may be the good Fortune of this. My respectful Compliments to Mrs Hancock and believe me to be with very great Esteem,

Sir,
Your most Obedient humble Serv.t
B Franklin

T. Hancock Esqr

> We whose Names are hereunto subscribed, taking into Consideration, that in the Library of the College at Cambridge in New England, many Books useful to Students in the several Branches of Learning are yet wanting; and that as new Improvements are from time to time made in Science, new Books on new Subjects are continually coming forth, with which Seminaries of Learning especially should be early furnished, for the further Qualification of the Tutors, and Advantage of the Youth by them to be instructed: But inasmuch as there is not yet any Fund for such Purposes belonging to the said College, therefore to remedy that Deficiency in some degree for the Present, and farther to advance the Reputation of the College and the Public Good; WE do each of us promise to pay Annually for Five Years to come, the Sums to our respective Names annexed, into the Hands of the Treasurer of the said College for the Time being, to be disposed of in the Purchase of such Books for the Library, as the President and Fellows shall from time to time order and direct.

Time of Subscribing	Names of Subscribers	Annual Subscript. for Five Years	Lawful Money £ s d
Sept. 11. 1755	Benj. Franklin of Philadelph.	Four Pistoles	4 8 0

NO. 19 Benjamin Franklin wrote to Thomas Hancock to suggest that he encourage friends of the Harvard College library to establish a purchase fund. He enclosed a subscription form (illustrated above) on which he listed his own annual pledge of four pistoles. A draft for the first installment (illustrated overleaf) accompanied the form, but was never submitted for payment — thus a most charming document remains in the Harvard College library.

Philad. Sept. 11. 1755

Sir,

Pay to the Treasurer of Harvard College for the time being, Four Pistoles, or Four Pound Eight Shillings Lawful Money, being my Subscription to the Library of the said College for one Year next ensuing the Date hereof, and charge the same to Acc.t of

Your Loving Brother
B Franklin

To Mr John Franklin
Post m.r Boston

When the troops which the British sent to stop the marauding French and Indians met ignominious defeat, the Pennsylvanians set about defending themselves. In January, 1756, Franklin successfully led three hundred volunteers to fortify the towns on the western frontier and to organize local militia — thereby adding to his many roles that of military commander.

Problems with the enemy were compounded by the Proprietors — founder William Penn's sons and heirs — who insisted that their vast land holdings should remain exempt from taxation; thus refusing, in effect, to pay their share for defense. Franklin was delegated by the Assembly to present its case to the Crown, and to negotiate with the Penns. After a three-month delay in New York, he sailed for England on June 20, 1757. During the voyage his scientific curiosity was aroused by the variations in the ship's performance under the different officers commanding the watches, and he wrote in his *Autobiography* that "a set of experiments might be instituted" to study optimum hull design, rigging, setting of the sails, and lading. When not busy with scientific observations and speculations, he occupied himself by preparing the 1758 edition of *Poor Richard*, including the famous "Father Abraham's Speech" (NOS. 8 and 9).

In London he at last met Peter Collinson and William Strahan, with whom he had corresponded for so many years; and Dr. John Fothergill, editor of *Experiments and Observations*, who arranged a meeting with the Penn family. Negotiations went slowly and badly. Between rounds, Franklin travelled, and enjoyed the company of English scientists and printers. The institutions he had encouraged while at home continued in his benevolent interest during his absence, Harvard College among them.

On April 28, 1758, he wrote a very long letter to Thomas Hubbard, Treasurer of the College, to explain the workings of a thirty-five cell "battery" he was sending for Professor Winthrop (NO. 20). He closed with a postscript: "I beg the College will do me the favour to accept a Virgil I send in the

Case, thought to be the most curiously printed of any Book hitherto done in the World" (NO. 21).

This curious volume contained the *Bucolics, Georgics,* and *Æneid* printed by John Baskerville, a fellow printer whose innovations in typeface designs, inks and papers, together with meticulous presswork, were greatly admired by Franklin.

Thomas Hubbard soon received another letter from London, dated May 13, 1758 (NO. 22). It was from Joseph Mico, the agent who for years had kept Harvard's English accounts, receiving sums payable from legacies, remitting part to the Treasurer, and spending the rest as required for books and other supplies ordered by the College. He wrote:

> Sir.
> I have now before me, your favours of the 23d. January, & its copy, inclosing a Memorandum, for Benja. Franklin Esqr:, from Mr. Winthrop, Hollissian Professor of the Mathematicks, at Harvard College, & a few Lines from yourself, desiring him to procure a few Articles, for the use of said College, & to deliver them to me. That Memorandum was delivered him, & he sent me a Case, wth. Electrifying Instrumts. &ca., which I have shipt, & also a small Trunk of Hebrew Psalters &ca. . . . Inclosed is a Letter for yourself, from Mr. Franklin, which he delivered me open; I paid him £10.3.7 for the Things purchased by him, & have charged it in the above Invoice. . . .
>
> Sr: Your most humb. Servt.
> JOSEPH MICO.[16]

Franklin, too, was apparently acting as Harvard's agent in London, and was corresponding with Professor Winthrop, although only one of the letters written by Franklin to Winthrop during this stay in England has been found. It is preserved at the American Philosophical Society, and on it Winthrop drafted his reply, thanking Franklin for his "favor of 20 Feb. and 8 April last, the former inclosing Dr. Pringles paper on an extraordinary meteor, and the later Mr. Kennicotts papers relating to the Hebrew Bible." "Give me leave now sir to congratulate you on the honorary distinctions

P. VIRGILII MARONIS

AENEIDOS

LIBER PRIMUS.

I L L E *ego, qui quondam gracili modulatus avena*
Carmen ; *et egreſſus ſilvis, vicina coegi*
Ut quamvis avido parerent arva colono:
Gratum opus agricolis: at nunc horrentia Martis

5 A RMA, virumque cano, Trojæ qui primus ab oris
Italiam, fato profugus, Lavinaque venit
Litora: multum ille et terris jactatus et alto,
Vi ſuperum, ſævæ memorem Junonis ob iram:
Multa quoque et bello paſſus, dum conderet urbem,
10 Inferretque Deos Latio: genus unde Latinum,
Albanique patres, atque altæ moenia Romæ.
Muſa, mihi cauſas memora, quo numine læſo,
Quidve dolens Regina Deum, tot volvere caſus
Inſignem pietate virum, tot adire labores
15 Impulerit. tantæne animis coeleſtibus iræ?
Urbs antiqua fuit, Tyrii tenuere coloni,
Carthago, Italiam contra, Tiberinaque longe
Oſtia, dives opum, ſtudiiſque aſperrima belli:
Quam Juno fertur terris magis omnibus unam
20 Poſthabita coluiſſe Samo. hic illius arma,
Hic currus fuit: hoc regnum Dea gentibus eſſe,
O   Si

NO. 21 The opening verses of Virgil's Æneid, handsomely printed by John Baskerville in 1757, and presented to Harvard by Franklin.

conferred on you at home [Scotland!]," wrote Winthrop. "I shall look upon your correspondence as a great obligation, when you can find leisure to favor me with it."[17]

Franklin finally returned to Philadelphia in 1762, having at last reached a compromise with the Proprietors. There he learned of a disaster which struck Harvard during the night of January 24, 1764. Harvard Hall, where the General Court of Massachusetts was meeting to avoid the smallpox, then epidemic in Boston, was destroyed by fire, and with it the College library and scientific apparatus. The General Court appropriated funds to rebuild the hall, for which Governor Bernard supplied the plans, but the replacement of the library and apparatus was left to individual benefactors. Chief among these was Thomas Hollis, the second of that name to assist Harvard with generous donations of books and funds. It was he who paid for the apparatus which Franklin selected for Harvard when he returned to England, and which is the subject of several surviving letters to John Winthrop.

In the first of these letters, dated July 10, 1764, Franklin wrote, "I shall think of the Affair of your unfortunate College, and try if I can be of any Service in procuring some Assistance towards restoring your Library" (NO. 23).[18]

Four years later he begins a letter, "You must needs think the time long that your instruments have been in hand. Sundry circumstances have occasioned the delay."[19] Since his return to London in December, 1764, to petition the Crown to remove the Penns from Pennsylvania and to rule the Colony directly, he had resumed his informal post as purchasing agent for Harvard. The task of replacing the astronomical instruments Professor Winthrop had lost in the fire with the finest now obtainable turned out to be slow work indeed. Franklin's letter goes on to explain that James Short's progress on the telescope was interrupted first by his frequent bouts of illness, then by his death. But it was now almost complete, would soon be released by the executors of the estate, and was "much more valuable than it would have

NO. 23 Illustrated above are the opening and closing lines of Franklin's letter of July 10, 1764, to Professor Winthrop. It begins with congratulations on the recovery of the family from smallpox, continues with an appraisal of Æpinus's theory of magnetism, and closes with regrets over the loss of the College library and "respectful compliments" to his friends at Harvard.

been if he had lived, as he excelled all others in that branch" (NO. 24).

Franklin continues: "The equal altitudes and transit instrument was undertaken by Mr. Bird, who doing all his work with his own hands for the sake of greater truth and exactness, one must have patience that expects any thing from him." One's patience is further tried by the fact that Bird was sidetracked by orders from Russia and France for instruments required to observe the transit of Venus which would occur on June 3, 1769.

"Mr. Martin, when I called to see his panopticon, had not one ready." But Franklin is not discouraged, and in the meantime he is sending on behalf of Nevil Maskelyne, the astronomer royal, pamphlets of instructions for observing the upcoming transit of Venus. It is hoped that one of the Colonies will send an expedition to Lake Superior, where the entire transit will be visible.

James Bowdoin had used his influence as a member of the Council to persuade the General Court of Massachusetts to finance Winthrop's expedition to Newfoundland to study the transit of 1761. Winthrop's meticulous account of his methods and observations was welcomed by the Royal Society and by James Short, the telescope expert, who was assigned to compile the data received by all observers. Eight years later, opposition to the Townshend duties had left Massachusetts government a shambles and Bowdoin was unable to raise funds. Moreover, Winthrop was not well enough to travel. But in a letter to Franklin, which Franklin hand copied for the Royal Society, he explained for other observers the apparent time lapse aberrations in the transit, using ballistic analogs.

For the benefit of his students and others interested, Winthrop published *Two Lectures on the Parallax and Distance of the Sun as Deducible from the Transit of Venus*, in which he explained how records of the exact time of Venus's entering and leaving the sun's disc, computed from strategic locations around the earth, could be compiled to provide the

NO. 24 This telescope was constructed under Franklin's supervision by James Short, who was among the most skilled of England's telescope makers and an accomplished astronomer.

data necessary to determine the earth's distance from the sun. He explained the function of a meridian telescope and equal altitudes instrument, and noted that those used in Britain, France, and Russia were "all made by the accurate hand of Mr. Bird of London who also made the instrument of that kind which lately arrived here for the use of this College"[20] (NOS. 25 and 26).

On March 11, 1769, Franklin began a letter to Winthrop: "At length after much delay and Difficulty I have been able to obtain your Telescope that was made by Mr. Short before his Death"[21] (NO. 27). Having detailed the further problems with

NO. 25 This meridian telescope and equal altitudes instrument was made by John Bird for Professor Winthrop and his students.

that telescope, he wonders whether the College has yet received Mr. Bird's instrument "which went from hence in September per Capt. Watt." The comment in Professor Winthrop's *Lectures* suggests that it did, indeed, arrive in Cambridge, and although the meridian telescope and equal altitudes instrument still preserved at Harvard is unsigned, its construction and the documentary evidence all point to its being the one Franklin ordered from Bird.

On April 25, 1769, the President and Fellows of Harvard College voted:

> That the thanks of this Board be given to Dr. Franklin for his many very obliging acts of friendship; particularly for his care in procuring several valuable Instruments for the Apparatus, and that he be desired to continue his kind regards to the College.[22]

The "several valuable Instruments" must be a reference to those Franklin discussed in his letter of July, 1768: the Short telescope and Bird equal altitudes instrument still at Harvard, and the Martin "Panopticon," whereabouts unknown. The reference may also be to some of the instruments in the large shipments dispatched by Joseph Mico in response to orders placed by the College treasurer, Thomas Hubbard. Several of the London instrument makers were knowledgeable scientists and it is quite possible that as Franklin browsed about their shops he chatted with them and made suggestions as to what instruments would be best for Harvard.

That he dealt with Benjamin Martin we know. Martin was the author of numerous books on science, including *The Young Gentleman and Lady's Philosophy* . . .(NO. 28), and made apparatus for demonstrations and experiments in many branches of natural philosophy. Among the numerous examples of his work still at Harvard is a set of weights and pulleys which was part of a consignment listed on Mico's invoice of September 24-25, 1765 (NO. 29). Professor Winthrop would have demonstrated with these when he lectured on

NO. 28 Frontispiece to *The Young Gentleman and Lady's Philosophy, . . . Containing a Philosophy of the Heavens*, by Benjamin Martin.

A PERSPECTIVE 65

NO. 29 Benjamin Martin made this set of weights and pulleys for Professor Winthrop's classroom demonstrations.

the pulley. His lectures on electricity would have been accompanied by demonstrations using one of the College's electrostatic machines, which are unsigned, but were part of a shipment in which all other items were from Martin's shop (NO. 30). The world's foremost electrician may well have had a hand in selecting these machines for the College to which more than ten years earlier he had sent, via James Bowdoin, a dozen Leyden jars.

The "Summary of a Course of Experimental Philosophical Lectures," which was "Concluded on the 16th of June 1746, by Mr. John Winthrop" — a small notebook preserved in the Harvard College Library — records the curriculum served by

NO. 30 Lectures on electricity were enlivened with sparks from this electrostatic machine, which probably came from Martin's shop.

all this equipment (NO. 31). The final lecture offered some instruction in astronomy, beginning with the planetary orbits; "The Rest of this Lecture was on the Orary, a Machine Whereon was admirably Shown the motion of the Moon around the Earth, and of both round the Sun, as their Center."[23]

After 1768 the students could study a very admirable orrery indeed. It is inscribed, "Made & Improv'd/by B. MARTIN in/Fleet Street LONDON./The Gift of the/Honble. JAMES BOWDOIN Esq./To the Apparatus of Harvard College/ N.E. May 1764" (NO. 32). It was, in fact, Bowdoin's gift of £50 which was made in May, 1764. During the next three years

NO. 32 Astronomy was taught with the aid of this orrery made by Benjamin Martin. It was given to Harvard by James Bowdoin.

Mico forwarded, to Thomas Hubbard, Martin's endless excuses for the delays, and assurances that completion was near. Finally Mico could forward the orrery, but the bill was nearly double the £50 given by Bowdoin. Martin explained that it was Professor Winthrop's exacting specifications which brought the final cost so far above the estimate. Bowdoin graciously made up the difference.

Although Franklin had been sent to England in 1764 to petition the Crown for relief from the arbitrary rule of the Proprietors in Pennsylvania, he soon became the unofficial spokesman for all the Colonies in their protest against arbitrary taxation. During a turbulent period of British politics there was one minister who understood and championed the American point of view: William Pitt, Earl of Chatham. On January 4, 1769, the President and Fellows of Harvard College voted: "That the thanks of this Board be given to Dr. Benja. Franklin for his very acceptable present of a fine Bust, of that great assertor of American liberties, Lord Chatham."[24]

This plaster copy after the marble likeness by Joseph Wilton, R.A., was almost certainly the first sculpture to come into the possession of the College (NO. 33). It was displayed in the new Harvard Hall, with paintings of King George, Queen Charlotte and Governor Bernard. Of this group, it alone survived the Revolution.

The letter Franklin sent Winthrop on March 11, 1769, wondering whether Bird's transit instrument had arrived, tells of another consignment: "By a late Ship, I sent your College a Copy of the new Edition of my Philosophical Papers; and others I think for yourself and for Mr. Bowdoin. I should apologize to you for inserting therin some part of our Correspondence with out first obtaining your Permission: But as Mr. Bowdoin had favour'd me with his Consent, for what related to him; I ventur'd to rely on your Good Nature as to what related to you, and I hope you will forgive me."[25]

NO. 33 The plaster bust illustrated on the opposite page has been at Harvard more than two hundred years. The first sculpture in the College's collection of portraits, it is a likeness of William Pitt, Earl of Chatham, who, during the years of growing tension prior to the Revolution, urged that Parliament try to understand the American point of view. On December 11, 1777, Franklin wrote to Thomas Walpole: "I am sorry Lord Chatham's Motion for a Cessation of Arms, was not agreed to. . . . Blessed are the Peacemakers."

This edition of *Experiments and Observations on Electricity* ... was the first to be printed under Franklin's supervision (NO. 34). The letters he had received from Bowdoin in 1751 and 1752 were among those from New England friends which he incorporated. (See end note 9.)

Franklin's primary mission in England, to reconcile the government's view of the Colonies with the Colonies' view of themselves, is recalled in the postscript: "There is no Prospect of getting the Duty Acts repeal'd this Session if ever. Your steady Resolutions to consume no more British Goods may possibly if persisted in have a good Effect another Year. I apprehend the Parliamentary Resolves and Address will tend to widen the Breach."[26] In other words, the Colonies may best cope with Parliament's punitive resolutions by continuing their boycott of British manufactures. The British merchants thus threatened with financial ruin will join the Colonies in pleading for repeal of controversial taxes and enforcement measures. In the meantime, an intransigent Parliament is making reconciliation nearly impossible.

On June 6, 1770, Franklin again wrote to Winthrop about a number of subjects: the publication of the professor's transit observations; an achromatic telescope and some lenses which had been subject to the usual delays; lightning rod installation; and a curious phenomenon – "Towards the Beginning of last Winter Spots were seen in the Sun here by the naked Eyes of Multitudes of People, the Streets being full of Gazers for several Hours. The Smoke of the Town serv'd the purpose of colour'd Glasses."[27] Franklin was appalled by the air pollution. Perhaps Winthrop was too, but he must certainly have been interested in the sunspots since he had been observing them since 1739, and was, apparently, the first Colonial astronomer to do so.

Winthrop's reply, dated Cambridge, October 26, 1770, also covers several topics, and continues on the subject of lightning rods. "A little piece I inserted in our news papers last summer induced the people of Waltham (a town a few miles from hence), to fix rods upon their steeple, which had

166   LETTERS *and* PAPERS.

Extract of a Letter from a Gentleman in BOSTON, *to* BENJAMIN FRANKLIN, *Esq; concerning the* crooked Direction, *and the* Source *of* Lightning.

S I R,   *Boston, Dec.* 21, 1751.

THE experiments Mr *K*. has exhibited here, have been greatly pleasing to all sorts of people that have seen them; and I hope, by the time he returns to *Philadelphia*, his tour this way will turn to good account. His experiments are very curious, and I think prove most effectually your doctrine of Electricity; that it is a real element, annexed to, and diffused among all bodies we are acquainted with; that it differs in nothing from lightning, the effects of both being similar, and their properties, so far as they are known, the same, &c.

The remarkable effect of lightning on iron, lately discovered, in giving it the magnetic virtue, and the same effect produced on small needles by the electrical fire, is a further and convincing proof that they are both the same element; but, which is very unaccountable, Mr *K*. tells me, it is necessary to produce this effect, that the direction of the needle and the electric fire should be North and South; from either to the other, and that just so far as they deviate therefrom, the magnetic power in the needle is less, till their direction being at right angles with the North and South, the effect entirely ceases. We made at *Faneuil Hall*,

NO. 34 *Experiments and Observations on Electricity, Made at Philadelphia in America . . . To Which Are Added, Letters and Papers on Philosophical Subjects . . .,* including this report from James Bowdoin on Kinnersley's demonstrations at Faneuil Hall.

just before been much shattered and set on fire by lightning. They are now becoming pretty common among us, and numbers of people convinced of their efficacy."[28] Winthrop is preaching Franklin's message with Franklin's method.

Franklin replied in turn on February 5, 1771. He is sending Winthrop various publications, including the Royal Society's latest *Transactions,* and at long last the achromatic telescope and lenses. "I send also a present to the College Library two volumes 4to of a very learned work lately printed — Hoogevee on the Greek Particles: and two Mathematical Pieces of Mr. Masere, late Attorney General at Quebec, which I hope will be acceptable to the President and Corporation, whom I highly respect and honor. The print you mention is with the books."[29]

These books on the use of the negative sign in algebra, plane trigonometry, and some niceties of Greek grammar are still in the Library, as is the print (NOS. 35 and 36). It is a mezzotint by Edward Fisher after Mason Chamberlin's famous painting of 1762, and the engraver has emphasized all the melodramatic electrical iconography of the original. Franklin sits writing in his study, his attention distracted by the bells he has rigged up to signal impending electrical storms. Through his window one sees the sky illumined both by lightning bolts and by the conflagration which consumes the dwellings of those who have failed to put up lightning rods: "dwellings" which on close examination are the little models Franklin used to demonstrate the function of lightning rods. Franklin liked the print and sent impressions to many of his friends, including Mather Byles and John Winthrop.

At the end of his February, 1771, letter to Winthrop, Franklin writes that he has "nothing new in Astronomy or Natural Philosophy to communicate. . . . Dr. Priestley is about to publish a History of the latter, in the manner of his History of Electricity — it will make several volumes in quarto."[30] This ambitious undertaking, for which Priestley had sent an outline to Franklin, was never completed (NO. 57).

NO. 57 Joseph Priestley was a Nonconformist minister with a passion for experimental chemistry. He was fascinated by the properties of oxygen, which he called "dephlogisticated air," and in August, 1774, he prepared a sample of the gas. Politically liberal, he was openly sympathetic first to the American Revolution, then to the French. A mob sacked his house in 1791, and three years later, tired of being harassed for his unpopular views, he emigrated to Pennsylvania.

In June, 1771, the Corporation voted that Professor Winthrop transmit to Dr. Franklin their thanks for the Maseres, Hoogeveen and the print. A year later thanks were similarly voted for "a late valuable Work of Dr. Priestley entitled the History & Present State of the Discoveries relating to Vision, Light & Colours."[31] If the legend on the bookplate is correct, Franklin at the same time sent Priestley's earlier *The History and Present State of Electricity, with Original Experiments* (NO. 37). This volume contains a history of electricity prior to Franklin; Franklin's discoveries; subsequent developments; statements of electrical theories; and information on the construction and operation of "electrical machines."

In his preface Priestley notes that electrostatic machines, air pumps, and the like "exhibit the operations of nature" whereas globes and orreries "are only the means that ingenious men have hit upon to explain their own conception of things to others." Indeed, this prefatory essay is a most interesting statement of how a natural philosopher (scientist) working in the latter half of the eighteenth century perceived his rôle. Priestley compares and contrasts the pleasures afforded by the study of civil, natural and philosophical history. "Philosophy exhibits the powers of nature, discovered and directed by human art. . . . It is here that we see the human understanding to its greatest advantage, grasping at the noblest objects, and increasing its own powers, by acquiring to itself the powers of nature, and directing them to the accomplishment of its own views; whereby the security, and happiness of mankind are daily improved. . . . Lastly, the investigation of the powers of nature, like the study of Natural History, is perpetually suggesting to us views of divine perfections and providence, which are both pleasing to the imagination and improving to the heart."[32]

Franklin and Priestley were close friends. Franklin must have taken pleasure in writing to John Winthrop on July 25, 1773, that "Dr. Priestley is now well provided for. Lord Shelburne is become his Patron, and desirous to have the Company of a Man of general Learning to read with him &

superintend the Education of his Children, has taken him from his congregation at Leeds, settled 300£ a Year upon him for Ten Years, and 200£ for life with a house to live in near his Country Seat. My Lord has a great Library there which the Doctor is now putting in Order & seems very happy in his new Situation.The learned Leisure he will now have, secure of a comfortable Subsistance, gives his Friends a pleasing Hope of many useful Works from his Pen."[33]

Franklin and his American correspondents, however, found less and less learned leisure as the political situation deteriorated beyond repair. News of the Boston Tea Party reached London on January 19, 1774, followed by Governor Hutchinson's account of the riotous behavior of Boston mobs. Franklin had represented the Massachusetts Assembly in London since 1770, and when on January 30, 1774, he attempted to present a petition from the Assembly to the Privy Council of Lord North, Alexander Wedderburn, the solicitor general, thwarted him with an hour-long harangue, laden with invective, intended to amuse their Lordships and to humiliate Franklin. Parliament rejected a conciliation plan proposed by William Pitt, and adopted the Punitive Acts — known in America as the Intolerable Acts. These dealt especially harshly with New England. On February 25, Franklin wrote to Bowdoin that this was because "other provinces have done as offensive things, but *Whiggism* is thought to be more thoroughly the principle in New England, and that is now an unpardonable sin."[34]

By then Franklin knew his ten-year-long mission of reconciliation was a failure and he got ready to return to America — a departure made still sadder by the fact that he was too late to see his wife again: she had died in December. He spent his last day in London with Joseph Priestley, selecting from American newspapers articles which would arouse sympathy for the Colonies when reprinted in England. Yet he must have realized the futility of this final effort, for Priestley recalled that "he was frequently not able to proceed for the tears literally running down his cheeks."[35]

He wrote to Priestley shortly after his arrival in Philadelphia, noting that while he was at sea the British had marched on the country folk, and were defeated in the skirmishes we refer to now as the Battles of Lexington and Concord. Meanwhile, he had enjoyed a tranquil crossing during which he "made a valuable philosophical discovery": the temperature readings he took in the ocean confirmed part of the course of the Gulf Stream.[36] He had arrived home the evening of May 5, 1775, "and the next morning was unanimously chosen by the Assembly of Pennsylvania, a delegate to the [Second Continental] Congress now sitting."[37]

He wrote again on July 7 to tell of the "perfidy" of General Gage, and of his own busy schedule. "In the morning at six, I am at the Committee of Safety, appointed by the Assembly to put the province in a state of defence; which committee holds till near nine, when I am at the Congress, and that sits till after four in the afternoon." Franklin will "communicate [Priestley's] letter to Mr. Winthrop; but the camp is at Cambridge, and he has as little leisure for philosophy as myself."[38]

On October 3 he wrote Priestley that he was "to set out to-morrow for the camp,"[39] as one of the three appointees of the Continental Congress to discuss with George Washington the reorganization and provisioning of the Continental Army. Cambridge was no longer the community of scholars he had visited in 1753, for the College had evacuated to Concord, and American troops were billeted in the buildings of Harvard Yard. Boston was occupied by the British, so he would have been unable to visit any relatives still there. Those with whom he corresponded most frequently had fled to Rhode Island.

A letter written December 9, 1775, from Philadelphia to his friend Charles G. F. Dumas thanks him for his letters, and for three copies of Emmerich de Vattel's *Le Droit des Gens* . . . (NO. 38). "It came to us in good season, when the circumstances of a rising State make it necessary frequently to consult the law of nations. Accordingly, that copy which I kept, (after depositing one in our own public library here, and sending the other to the College of Massachusetts Bay, as you directed), has been continually in the hands of the members of our Congress, now sitting, who are much pleased with your notes and preface."[40]

On September 30, 1776, the President and Fellows of "the College of Massachusetts Bay" were back in Cambridge, meeting at the president's house, and voting that James Bowdoin, who had forwarded to them M. de Vattel's *Le Droit des Gens*, convey to Dr. Franklin their thanks for same.[41] The credit due M. Dumas seems to have been lost in the confusion of the war.

As Franklin was acquainted with more Europeans than any other American, he acted as chairman of the Secret Committee of Foreign Correspondence, to which he had been appointed by Congress. The body of his letter of December 9, 1775, to Dumas is an inquiry as to whether "if, as it seems likely to happen, we should . . . declare ourselves an independent people, there is any state or power in Europe, who would be willing to enter into an alliance with us for the benefit of our commerce." The Colonies are firmly united with a good army, "yet both arms and ammunition are much wanted. Any merchants, who would venture to send ships laden with those articles, might make a great profit." Also required are two good engineers, "one acquainted with field service, sieges, &c., and the other with fortifying seaports."[42]

In March, 1776, Franklin was again one of three men appointed to journey north, this time to Canada to raise support for the American cause among French Canadians. The trip was too much for a man of seventy; he became so ill and exhausted that he wrote letters of farewell to a number of friends. But Philip Schuyler of Albany, and his family, nursed him back to stability, if not health, and he proceeded on to Canada. To protect against the biting cold he bought the marten fur cap which would soon be a sensation in Paris. But the French in Canada stood firm in their isolationism. He returned to Philadelphia, and there contributed as much as his strength would permit to Thomas Jefferson's draft of the Declaration of Independence.

Franklin's health gradually improved, and on October 26, 1776, he sailed for France to negotiate for aid and an alliance — again as one of three commissioners appointed by Congress (NO. 39). But his own renown as a philosopher was far greater than any prestige he might have had as the emissary of the rebellious Colonies. For this reason he pled the American cause with his friends among the intelligentsia as well as through representatives of the government; this may also account for his decision not to abandon the comfortable dress of the Pennsylvania savant for that of a statesman. The venerable philosopher who went about under a fur cap rather than a wig became a symbol of liberty. Well before Louis XVI and his advisers decided it would be a sound financial risk to join the Americans to discomfit the British, Franklin was a popular hero in France: Bonhomme Richard of the *Almanack* and lightning rod.

This popularity was enhanced by a project of Jacques Donatien Le Ray de Chaumont, the friend who provided him with a house at Passy. Le Ray had acquired the historic château at Chaumont in 1750, and had established there a pottery and glassmaking center. Under his direction, Jean-Baptiste Nini, the Italian sculptor and engraver who was manager of the pottery works, produced on a terra cotta medallion a profile portrait of the old man in the fur cap, identified concisely but adequately as ".B·FRANKLIN. .AMERICAIN." On the *tranche* of the shoulder are impressed "NINI/F 1777"; and in relief is a fanciful device consisting of a crowned shield emblazoned with thunderbolt and lightning rod (NO. 40).

These medallions must have been in circulation by June 17, 1777, when Franklin mentions them in a letter. On December 11 he wrote to Thomas Walpole that "from a Sketch . . . drawn by your ingenious and valuable Son, they have made here Medallions in *terre cuit*. A Dozen have been presented to me, and I think he has a Right to one of them."[43]

NO. 40 Benjamin Franklin, as portrayed in the first of a series of terra-cotta reliefs modelled by Jean-Baptiste Nini.

Young Walpole, then, had made the original portrait drawing. Perhaps it included the fur hat as rendered in the Nini medallion, which is less a representation of Franklin's cap than of one worn by the French philosopher Jean Jacques Rousseau in a popular print. A more accurate delineation of

NO. 41 Augustin de Saint Aubin's likeness of Benjamin Franklin, after a drawing by Charles Nicolas Cochin, the younger.

the Canadian cap is given in an engraving by Augustin de Saint Aubin after a drawing by Charles Nicholas Cochin, which was issued on June 16, 1777 — just about the time the Nini medallion appeared. The legend, "BENJAMIN FRANKLIN./ Né à Boston, dans la nouvelle Angleterre le 17. Janvier 1706.," is more explicit than Nini's in identifying the New World origins of the wise old man (NO. 41).

The Saint Aubin/Cochin likeness shows Franklin wearing his spectacles, and Nini included them in one version of the terra-cotta medallion (NO. 42). Among the several other variations he modelled are three based on a drawing by Anne Vallayer-Coster, a friend of Beaumarchais and the American cause. These were issued in 1778 and 1779, after Franklin had finally negotiated a Franco-American alliance. Franklin, now minister plenipotentiary for the United States of America to the Court of France, is depicted in the classical style befitting a dignitary. In Latin, Turgot's epigram, "ERIPUIT COELO FULMEN SCEPTRUMQUE TIRANNIS," proclaims his preeminence

NO. 42 In this version, Nini left on Franklin's spectacles.

both as scientist and statesman.[44] The decorative elements which separate the words comprise the cloud from which descends a lightning bolt, and the hand holding a lightning rod (!) with which Nini charged the arms he invented for Franklin. The legends on some of Nini's medallions portraying French nobility are similarly divided by the charges of their arms (NO. 43).

Le Ray du Chaumont followed his medallion project with a commission to Joseph Siffred Duplessis, the best of the court portraitists, to paint a likeness of Franklin for his own collection. It was exhibited at the Salon of 1779, where it attracted the enthusiastic approbation of crowds of visitors. The American hero was presented to the French public in a frame magnificently carved with the attributes of Liberty, Peace, and Victory, and identified by a single word: VIR. There was a tremendous demand for copies of the portrait. More than twenty years later, long after the upheavals of France's own revolution had left him nearly penniless, Duplessis was exhibiting a late replica at the Salon of 1801. How

NO. 43 Nini medallion after a drawing by Anne Vallayer-Coster.

many replicas he made, to what extent his workshop assisted, how many copies were painted by others are not known (NO. 44). Only the great painting exhibited in 1779 is signed. Today it hangs in the Metropolitan Museum of Art.

An engraving made by Juste Chevillet (1729-90) soon after the completion of the painting in 1778 sold a large edition

NO. 44 Benjamin Franklin, by Joseph-Siffred Duplessis.

NO. 46 NO. 47

(NO. 45). In 1782 Joseph Wright (1756-93) painted an amended copy of Duplessis's pastel version of the portrait. This painting was the source of numerous further copies made for both English and American patrons.

Franklin's appearance at the time of his French mission is recorded also in two terra-cotta busts: a life portrait modelled by Jean Jacques Caffiéri in 1777 and exhibited at the Salon the following year; and a bust signed by Jean Antoine Houdon in 1778, which was exhibited at the same Salon — 1779 — as the Duplessis painting. The numerous casts taken from each served as models for the many artists who produced Franklin's likeness for years to come, not only in marble, porcelain, bronze, and silver, but in virtually all media from engravings to painted cups. Caffiéri was able to arrange sittings with Franklin, and his stern portrait is undoubtedly the more physiognomically correct of the two (NO. 46). Houdon was acquainted with Franklin through their

NO. 48   NO. 49

fraternal and social activities, and is believed to have modelled his bust from memory and, perhaps, informal sketches. The result is a portrait more animated than the careful study of his older rival (NO. 47).

Both busts were reproduced in unglazed porcelain, the Caffiéri with variations, by the royal porcelain manufactory at Sèvres. The very large coat buttons popular in the 1790s, which appear in one version of the Caffiéri, strongly suggest that it was one of the many French tributes to Franklin after his death (NO. 48). A small silver bust at the Fogg Art Museum also derives from the Caffiéri portrait, and appears to be a memorial (NO. 49).

Another example of such posthumous likenesses is the terra-cotta statuette exhibited by François Marie Suzanne at the Salon of 1793. Tremendously popular, it was soon reproduced in marble, plaster, bronze and other metals, and finally made its way to England as the figure of the all-American hero, serving the Staffordshire chinamakers as "General Washington" (NOS. 50 and 51).

A curious miniature at the Fogg Art Museum may also be posthumous (NO. 52). The costume clearly derives from the portrait painted in 1778 or 1779 by Anne Rosalie Filleul, one of the circle of young women who charmed and were

NO. 50 Franklin, after Suzanne's terra-cotta statuette of 1793.
NO. 51 Inscription notwithstanding, Franklin after Suzanne.

charmed by Franklin. The treatment of the head and the oval format suggest that the immediate source was an engraving made by an unknown artist in 1780, showing Diogenes having found an honest man — or, at least, having found Benjamin Franklin as depicted by Madame Filleul (NO. 53).[45]

In spite of the war, there continued in England a market

NO. 52 Miniature portrait of Benjamin Franklin, after Anne Rosalie Filleul, by way of "N. L. G. D. L. C. A. D. L."

NO. 53 The yoke is broken, the eagle rises phoenix-like from the lightning and flames that consume a map of America, the dove of peace wings skyward, and Diogenes displays the portrait of an honest man.

for small likenesses of Franklin. Most popular were the small stoneware medallions manufactured by his friend and admirer, Josiah Wedgwood. The two men had much in common, including the circumstances of their childhood. Wedgwood was born in 1730, the youngest of twelve children. Like Franklin, he was apprenticed to an older brother. Having learned the family craft of pottery, he entered into two brief partnerships during which he experimented with various bodies and glazes. He was always watchful for a way to improve his product — and the means of its production. He promoted the construction of turnpikes and of the Trent and Mersey Canal to facilitate the transportation of both his raw materials and finished wares. It was while preparing a pamphlet advocating the canal that he became a friend of Dr. Erasmus Darwin, with whom he subsequently collaborated on scientific experiments ranging from improvements for windmills to electric therapy for paralysis. A happy consequence of their long friendship was the marriage of Wedgwood's daughter and Darwin's son, the parents of Charles Darwin.

A good scientist — perhaps the first who may be properly called an industrial chemist — Wedgwood became the friend and frequent correspondent of Joseph Priestley, for whom he made such chemical apparatus as retorts, crucibles, pestles and mortars (NO. 57). Priestley was interested in Wedgwood's experiments with clays and glazes — including an unsuccessful search for a leadless glaze after he had been alerted to the dangers of lead poisoning — and suggested that he might in some way employ an electrical process to decorate teaware. It was Priestley who sent Wedgwood's paper on the pyrometer — a thermometer he had invented which would register in heat too high for mercurial thermometers — to Joseph Banks, president of the Royal Society. The membership heard it with approbation, and the following January, 1783, elected him a Fellow.

Wedgwood's closest friend was Thomas Bentley, with whom he signed a partnership agreement in 1769 for the manufacture and sale of ornamental ware — neoclassical vases and plaques, intaglios, and portrait medallions, as distinct from useful tableware. After much experimenting Wedgwood had developed a material suitable for these ornamental pieces, a fine black stoneware he later referred to as "basaltes." In 1775 his continued research was rewarded with the discovery of a new ceramic body, white and colored jasper. This became the most popular material for the ornamental ware, and portrait medallions made from it were in wide demand. Franklin was one of Wedgwood's earliest subjects. Creamware and basalt medallions modelled after a wax profile portrait by Isaac Gosset may have been made as early as 1768. In 1777 Wedgwood issued a reproduction of the first Nini "fur hat" medallion, and the following year he copied the Sèvres medallion. About the same time the firm began production of an original design in eight sizes, ranging from an eleven by eight-inch plaque to a cameo for setting in a ring. It was probably modelled by Hackwood, one of Wedgwood's more able sculptors, who began work with the firm as a boy and remained sixty-three years. The earliest examples of the two and a half by two-inch size were stamped "Dr. FRANKLIN," and on August 24, 1778, Wedgwood wrote to Thomas Bentley, "The Dr. before Franklin was an error which I corrected as soon as I saw it."[46] But one example, at least, went into circulation and is now at the Fogg Museum (NO. 54).

About the time Wedgwood perfected the composition of jasper he began to envision the expansion of the portrait medallion into a series of "Illustrious Moderns" (NOS 55-76). Among the medallions produced for this project are the likenesses of many of Franklin's friends, associates, and adversaries, a good number of whom he shared with Wedgwood, who was an ardent supporter of the Americans. On March 3, 1778, he wrote to Thomas Bentley lamenting "the present most wicked and preposterous war with our brethren and best friends."[47]

A month before Wedgwood wrote these words, on February 6, Franklin and his fellow commissioners, Arthur Lee and Silas Deane, had signed a treaty of alliance and commerce with the French. There was, however, little harmony among the commissioners. Neither Lee nor Deane was blessed with a diplomat's temperament, and the Continental Congress, alarmed at reports of their quarrels, recalled Deane. His return to Philadelphia was less a disgrace than a triumph, for he arrived escorting Conrad Alexander Gérard, France's newly appointed ambassador to America. This further angered Lee, who continued to send a stream of contentious letters to Franklin (NO. 78).

John Adams replaced Silas Deane as the third commissioner, but the acrimony between Franklin and Lee only increased. Congress finally realized the troika arrangement was unworkable, and early in 1779 appointed Franklin as minister plenipotentiary to the Court of France. This meant, however, that he was not only sole negotiator with the French, but sole trouble-shooter for overseas Americans, including prisoners held by the British, whose miserable lot he

NO. 54 Medallion of Franklin issued by his friend, Josiah Wedgwood.

did his best to ameliorate. But his major concern was to convince his French friends and the government to continue supplying arms, uniforms, and money, and to keep their faith in America's fragile credit (NO. 79).

Arthur Lee, meanwhile, was back in Philadelphia, and, with others opposed to Franklin, was attacking him in Congress. Franklin, exhausted with work and crippled with gout, offered his resignation. Congress refused to accept it, and Franklin continued at his post, searching for additional financing. The French government was nearly bankrupt, and unable to help. Fortunately, on October 17, 1781, the British under Cornwallis were defeated by the Americans, led by Washington, and their French allies under Lafayette and Rochambeau (NO. 80).

On April 8, 1782, Franklin wrote to Washington:

> I have heretofore congratulated your Excellency on your victories over our enemy's generals; I can now do the same on your having overthrown their politicians. Your late successes have so strengthened the hands of opposition in Parliament, that they are become the majority, and have compelled the King to dismiss all his old ministers and their adherents. The unclean spirits he was possessed with are now cast out of him; but it is imagined, that, as soon as he has obtained a peace, they will return with others worse than themselves, *and the last state of that man,* as the Scripture says, *shall be worse than the first.*[48]

Lord Rockingham, who had assisted Franklin in presenting to Parliament the reasons for American opposition to the Stamp Act, was again prime minister. Lord Shelburne, another supporter of the Americans and former friend of Franklin, was secretary of state for American affairs. He sent Richard Oswald as his most trusted, personal representative to begin peace negotiations.

John Jay, John Adams, and Henry Laurens were appointed by Congress to join Franklin as the American peace commissioners. But it was not until January 20, 1783, that, together with France and Spain, they signed a cessation of arms

NO. 80 Portrait of George Washington, by C. W. Peale, 1784.

and preliminary peace agreement with England. Finally, on September 3, the official Treaty of Peace, which was essentially a restatement of the initial agreement, was signed in Paris.

In spite of Adams's vociferous mistrust of the French, Franklin managed to maintain the cordial Franco-American friendship reflected in the many French medals struck in honor of American independence. A number of these were designed by Franklin's friend Augustin Dupré, who signed a medal depicting Franklin "SCULPSIT ET DICAVIT/AUG. DUPRÉ": engraved and dedicated by Augustin Dupré[49] (NO. 81).

In October, 1783, Adams went to England (NO. 82), while Franklin remained at Passy, enjoying the company of his friends there, and from time to time participating in the scientific inquiries of his French colleagues. Ballooning had become a postwar craze, and Franklin sent to Sir Joseph Banks, president of the Royal Society, detailed accounts of the launchings he observed (NOS. 67 and 83). In 1784 he was among the eminent scientists appointed to a royal commission to determine the authenticity of the cures Friedrich Anton Mesmer claimed to achieve with magnetism. The committee found it was the patient's belief in the efficacy of the treatments, rather than the magnetism, which effected any cures. The implication of this finding for a new science of psychology was apparently unappreciated, and Mesmer was discredited.

Franklin finally sailed from Le Havre in July, 1785. During a four-day layover in Southampton, he was visited by several of his English friends, including Jonathan Shipley and his family, at whose home he had begun his *Autobiography*. To relieve his numerous ailments he bathed in a hot salt water pool, where he fell asleep on his back—a phenomenon he "should hardly have thought possible. Water is the easiest bed that can be."[50]

During the voyage to Philadelphia he busied himself as before with observations and reflections on maritime matters. These he recorded in a letter addressed to David Le Roy,

NO. 82 Portrait of John Adams, by John Singleton Copley, 1783.

NO. 67 Sir Joseph Banks, by John Flaxman for Wedgwood & Bentley.

which was printed in the *Transactions of The American Philosophical Society* the following year. He again speculated on using mathematical formulae and test models to improve hull and sail design. He proposed methods to better the construction of anchors. He wondered whether ships might be propelled with jets of pumped sea water. He continued his measurements of the temperature of the Gulf Stream, and compiled charts of these and earlier findings. He urged that all ship captains study Captain Cook's methods of provisioning ships with nourishing staples properly stored; and he wished that someone would manufacture seagoing soup tureens with many partitions, to prevent the soup from slopping about. Finally, digressing a bit from the subject of ships' stores, he lamented the high price of sugar – not only in currency, but in the blood and sweat and human lives with which the sugar islands, and the slaves who labored there, were conquered.

Franklin reached Philadelphia in mid-September, and had hardly disembarked before he was elected president of the Executive Council of Pennsylvania. Letters congratulating him on his safe return were received from old friends throughout the States, including James Bowdoin (NO. 84), to whom he replied:

> It gave me great Pleasure, my dear Friend, to receive your kind Letter of Congratulation, as it prov'd, that all my old Friends in Boston were not estranged from me by the malevolent Misrepresentations of my Conduct, that had been circulated there, but that one of the most esteemed still retained a Regard for me. Indeed, you are now almost the only one left me by nature; Death having, since we were last together, depriv'd me of my dear Cooper, Winthrop, and Quincy.[51]

Their renewed correspondence dealt sometimes with the publication of scientific papers, sometimes with political problems such as Shays's Rebellion. The suppression of this violent insurrection of destitute farmers from western Massachusetts was the most unpleasant duty Bowdoin had to perform as governor, and his fellow chief executive in Pennsylvania offered support. A year later, on May 31, 1788, Franklin wrote wistfully:

> Our ancient Correspondence used to have something Philosophical in it. As you are now more free from public Cares, and I expect to be so in a few Months, why may we not resume that kind of Correspondence? Our much regretted Friend˙Winthrop once made me the Compliment, that I was good at starting a Game for Philosophers; let me try if I can start a little for you.[52]

But political philosophy continued to demand what remained of Franklin's strength. From May until September, 1787, he attended the Constitutional Convention almost daily, as a delegate from Pennsylvania, and as architect of innumerable compromises. On the final day of the convention he gave an address — read for him since he was too ill to speak himself — pleading for the unanimous adoption of

NO. 84 Christian Gullager painted this posthumous portrait of Governor Bowdoin surveying the paraphernalia of his "Great Upper Chamber." At one time it contained some twelve hundred books, six telescopes, and a vast assortment of philosophical apparatus.

the Constitution: a less than perfect document, but one that embodied the best efforts of an assembly of honest mortals.

Soon after, he was returned for a third one-year term as president of the Executive Council of Pennsylvania. From the prestige of this office, and as president of the Pennsylvania Society for Promoting the Abolition of Slavery and the Relief of Free Negroes, he exerted all the pressure he could to halt the traffic in slaves. Further, he urged that freed negroes be given opportunities to learn trades at which they could earn their living.

Josiah Wedgwood was an active member of the Society for the Suppression of the Slave Trade, and from the committee's seal produced a cameo medallion modelled by William Hackwood. A manacled slave is encircled with the inscription, "AM I NOT A MAN AND A BROTHER?" On February 27, 1788, Wedgwood sent a number of the medallions to Franklin, to whom he wrote: "It gives me great pleasure to be embarked on this occasion in the same great and good cause with you, and I ardently hope for the final completion of our wishes"[53] (NO. 85).

NO. 85 Josiah Wedgwood issued these cameo medallions for distribution among fellow abolitionists, both in England and America.

Much of Franklin's time was taken up in correspondence with his numerous friends on both sides of the Atlantic, and with courtesies extended to those who hoped to join this throng. While in Paris he had written letters of introduction for many young men leaving for America. This was one of the tasks taken over by Thomas Jefferson, when he replaced Franklin as minister plenipotentiary to the Court of France. On August 6, 1787, he wrote to Franklin to introduce a Dr. Gibbons. "It is a tax to which your celebrity submits you. every man of the present age will wish to have the honor of having known, and been known to you" (NOS. 86 and 87).

NO. 86 Portrait of Thomas Jefferson, by Gilbert Stuart, 1805.

Franklin was also under pressure from his friends to complete his *Autobiography*, but he found little time. His bladder stone caused pain so excruciating he had at times to relieve it with opium, which impeded both his digestion and his thoughts. But during periods of remission he caught up on his correspondence, both writing letters of farewell and answering technical questions. His last extant letter was to Jefferson, now secretary of state, who had inquired about the exact boundary between Maine and Canada.

> I am perfectly clear in the remembrance that the map we used in tracing the boundary, was brought to the treaty by the commissioners from England, and that it was the same that was published by Mitchell above twenty years before. Having a copy of that map by me in loose sheets, I send you that sheet which contains the Bay of Passamaquoddy, where you will see that part of the boundary traced.[54]

Nine days later, on April 17, 1790, Benjamin Franklin died. Twenty thousand persons followed their countryman to his burial place at Christ Church, Philadelphia. Eulogies were spoken and printed throughout the United States. In France, where the Chamber of Deputies went into mourning for three days, memorial ceremonies were held by printers' associations, learned societies, and other groups of admirers. France's artists once again paid tribute to their American friend, with commemorative portraits and designs for memorials (NO. 88).

While those he left behind mourned, Franklin departed from this world rejoicing. Although he often expressed his regret that he would not live to see the future progress made possible by science, he wrote frequently and cheerfully about death. After his return to Philadelphia he wrote to Jonathan Shipley, one of the English friends who came to bid him farewell at Southampton:

> The Course of Nature must soon put a period to my present Mode of Existence. This I shall submit to with less Regret, as, having seen during a long Life a good deal of this World, I feel

NO. 88 Drawing for a proposed commemorative engraving.

a growing Curiosity to be acquainted with some other; and can cheerfully, with filial Confidence, resign my Spirit to the conduct of that great and good Parent of Mankind, who created it, and who has so graciously protected and prospered me from my Birth to the Present Hour.[55]

* * *

I was born in Boston, New England, and owe my first instructions in literature to the free grammar-schools established there. I therefore give one hundred pounds sterling to my executors, to be by them . . . put out to interest . . . which interest annually shall be laid out in silver medals, and given as honourary rewards annually by the directors of the said free schools. . . .[57]

The medals for which Franklin thus provided in his will continue to be awarded by Boston's high schools, and several recent recipients are attending Harvard College.

Legacies of one thousand pounds to Boston and Philadelphia were for loans at five percent interest to "young married artificers" to assist in establishing themselves in a trade. Franklin anticipated that the interest accruing on these revolving loans would eventually be sufficient to finance major public works. Here he was too optimistic, for defaulted loans and inflation have taken their toll. Nevertheless, this fund created by Franklin's will continues to this day, a small monetary counterpart of the legacy of institutions, inventions, discoveries and wisdom left to his successors in this world.

Notes

1 Benjamin Franklin, *Autobiography*. Unless otherwise noted, subsequent passages within quotation marks are also from the *Autobiography*. The title is not Franklin's, but that given by many publishers to the account of his life which Franklin began in 1771 while living with the family of Dr. Jonathan Shipley, Bishop of St Asaph. He recorded up to the year 1730, when the turbulence of the impending Revolution required him to devote all his energies to his role as statesman. He began to continue the narrative while minister to France, in 1784, but made little progress. After his return to Philadelphia in 1788 he brought the story up to 1757. No subsequent biographer has chronicled Franklin's first fifty years with such vigor.

The *Autobiography* was published first in French, in 1791. It was translated back into English for a 1793 edition. Not until 1817 was it published from a copy of Franklin's English manuscript. Finally, in 1867, John Bigelow, United States minister to France, located the original manuscript. As might be expected, this autograph is the liveliest of the English versions; it is the text for most editions published subsequent to Bigelow's discovery. The four most important versions may be compared in Max Farrand's *Benjamin Franklin's Memoirs, Parallel Text Edition* (see Bibliography).

2 Benjamin Franklin, *The Papers of Benjamin Franklin*, ed. Leonard W. Labaree (vols. 1-14) and William B. Willcox (vols. 15-18), 18 vols. to date (New Haven: Yale University Press, 1959-), 1:11-13; reprinted from *The New-England Courant*, April 16, 1722.

3 *Ibid.*, pp. 14-18; reprinted from *The New-England Courant*, May 14, 1722.

4 Charles Coleman Sellers, *Benjamin Franklin in Portraiture* (New

Haven: Yale University Press, 1962), pp. 24-25; R. Peter Mooz, *Philadelphia Painting and Printing, Exhibition Catalogue of the Pennsylvania Academy of the Fine Arts* (Philadelphia: 1971), cat. no. 10; idem, "Robert Feke: The Philadelphia Story," in *American Painting to 1776: A Reappraisal, Winterthur Conference Report*, ed. I.M.G. Quimby (1971), p.203.

5 *Papers of Benjamin Franklin*, 3:115-19; reprinted from *Experiments and Observations on Electricity, Made at Philadelphia in America by Benjamin Franklin* . . . (London: printed for D. Henry, 1769), pp. 1-2.

6 *Ibid.*, p. 171.

7 *Ibid.*, 4:367-69; reprinted from *The Pennsylvania Gazette*, October 19, 1752.

8 *Ibid.*, reprinted from *Poor Richard improved: Being an Almanack . . . for the Year 1753* . . . (Philadelphia: printed and sold by B. Franklin).

9 *Ibid.*, pp. 216-21; printed from the autograph letter now at the Massachusetts Historical Society; much of it appeared in the 1769 and 1774 editions of *Experiments and Observations* as "Extract of a Letter from a Gentleman in Boston, to Benjamin Franklin, Esq.; concerning the crooked Direction, and the Source of Lightning."

10 *Ibid.*, p. 446.

11 *Ibid.*, pp. 461-62.

12 *Ibid.*, p. 462.

13 College Book VII, p. 41 (Cambridge: Harvard University Archives); printed in William C. Lane, "Harvard College and Franklin," in *Transactions, Publications of the Colonial Society of Massachusetts* (1907), 10:230.

14 Benjamin Franklin, *The Writings of Benjamin Franklin*, ed. Albert Henry Smyth (New York: Macmillan, 1905-07), 9:656.

15 *Papers of Benjamin Franklin*, 6:180-81.

16 Harvard College Papers I, p. 194 (Cambridge: Harvard University Archives); printed in Lane, "Harvard College and Franklin," p. 234.

17 *Papers of Benjamin Franklin*, 9:385-86.

18 *Ibid.*, 11:254-55.

19 *Ibid.*, 15:166-72.

20 John Winthrop, *Two Lectures on the Parallax and Distance of the Sun as Deducible from the Transit of Venus* . . . (Boston: printed and sold by Edes and Gill 1769), p. 42n.

21 *Papers of Benjamin Franklin*, 16:65-67.

22 College Book VII, p. 308; printed in Lane, "Harvard College and Franklin," p. 237.

23 John Winthrop, *The summary of a course of experimental philosophical lectures* [1746] (manuscript, Cambridge: Harvard University Archives); printed in I. Bernard Cohen, *Some Early Tools of American Science* (Cambridge: Harvard University Press, 1950), p. 43.

24 College Book VII, p. 305; printed in Lane, Harvard College and Franklin," p. 236.

25 *Papers of Benjamin Franklin*, 16:66.

26 *Ibid.*, p. 67.

27 *Ibid.*, 17:158-59.

28 *Ibid.*, p. 263.

29 *Ibid.*, 18:30.

30 *Ibid.*, p. 31.

31 College Book VII, p. 368; printed in Lane, "Harvard College and Franklin," p. 238.

32 Joseph Priestley, *The History and Present State of Electricity, with Original Experiments* (London: printed for J. Dodsley, 1767), pp. iv-xi.

33 *Writings of Benjamin Franklin*, ed. Smyth, 6:106-07.

34 *Ibid.*, p. 309.

35 Thomas Fleming, ed., *Benjamin Franklin: A Biography in His Own Words* (New York: Harper & Row, 1972), p. 262.

36 In 1770 Franklin had written his cousin Timothy Folger, a Nantucket whaling captain, to ask him to plot the course of the Gulf Stream, and had had the General Post Office print a chart based on Folger's data. Now he could confirm the accuracy of parts of this chart.

37 *Writings of Benjamin Franklin*, ed. Smyth, 6:400.

38 *Ibid.*, pp. 408-10.

NOTES

39 *Ibid.*, pp. 429-30.

40 *Ibid.*, p. 432.

41 Lane, "Harvard College and Franklin," pp. 238-39.

42 *Writings of Benjamin Franklin,* ed. Smyth, pp. 433-36.

43 Sellers, *Benjamin Franklin in Portraiture,* p. 345; pl. 10.

44 *Ibid.*, pp. 105-07, 347-48; pl. 11 (n.b. caption reversed with that of adjacent medallion).

45 *Ibid.*, pp. 281-84; pl. 23.

46 *Ibid.*, p. 397.

47 Ann Finer and George Savage, *The Selected Letters of Josiah Wedgwood* (New York: Born & Hawes, 1965), p. 217.

48 *Writings of Benjamin Franklin,* ed. Smyth, 8:420.

49 Sellers, *Benjamin Franklin in Portraiture,* pp. 275-77; pl. 20.

50 Fleming, *Benjamin Franklin,* p. 369.

51 *Writings of Benjamin Franklin,* ed. Smyth, 9:478

52 *Ibid.*, p. 652.

53 Finer and Savage, *Josiah Wedgwood,* p. 311.

54 *Writings of Benjamin Franklin,* ed. Smyth, 10:93.

55 *Ibid.*, 9:491.

56 *Ibid.*, p. 499.

The Catalogue

Many of the objects described in this catalogue have been lent to the Fogg Museum for this exhibition. Where no lender is specified, works of art are from the Museum's own collection.

1 *The New-England Courant*, No. 41

   Boston: 14 May 1722.   H. 30.5 x 20.5 cm.
   Courtesy of The Massachusetts Historical Society.

2 [Wollaston, William (1660-1724)]
   The Religion of Nature Delineated

   London: S. Palmer, 1724.   H. 25.5 cm.
   Lent by The Houghton Library; gift of friends, 1905, from the Library of Charles Eliot Norton.   Phil 8602.11.2.5*

3 Thévenot, Melchisédech (1620?-1692)
   L'Art de Nager Demontré par Figures . . .

   Paris: T. Moette, 1696.   H. 15 cm.
   Lent by The Houghton Library; deposited by Philip Hofer, 1967.
      *H615-212

4 Franklin, Benjamin
   The Art of Swimming, Made Safe, Easy, Pleasant, and Healthful . . .

   London: J. Fairburn [1829?].   H. 19 cm.
   Lent by The Houghton Library; gift of W. B. O. Field, 1944.
      *44W-1130

5 [Franklin, Benjamin]
Poor Richard Improved: Being an Almanack and Ephemeris . . . for the . . . year, 1748 . . . By Richard Saunders, Philom. [pseud.]
Philadelphia: B. Franklin [1747]. H. 16 cm.
Lent by The Houghton Library; gift in memory of Professor and Mrs. A. L. Rotch, 1942. *42-660

6 [Franklin, Benjamin]
Poor Richard Improved: Being an Almanack and Ephemeris . . . for the year . . . 1752 . . . By Richard Saunders, Philom. [pseud.]
Philadelphia: B. Franklin and D. Hall [1751]. H. 16.5 cm.
Lent by The Houghton Library; gift in memory of Professor and Mrs. A. L. Rotch, 1942. *42-661

7 [Franklin, Benjamin]
Poor Richard Improved: Being an Almanack and Ephemeris . . . for the year . . . 1754 . . . By Richard Saunders, Philom. [pseud.]
Philadelphia: B. Franklin and D. Hall [1753]. H. 16 cm.
Lent by The Houghton Library; gift in memory of Professor and Mrs. A. L. Rotch, 1942. *42-662

8 Franklin, Benjamin
The Way to Wealth
[London, 1779] broadside. H. 40.5 x 32 cm.
Lent by The Houghton Library; gift of David P. Wheatland, 1949. *49-203

9 [Franklin, Benjamin]
La Science du Bonhomme Richard . . .
Paris: Ruault, Libraire, 1777; Philadelphia. H. 17 cm.
Lent by The Houghton Library; Amy Lowell fund, 1961. x61-158

10 Cicero, Marcus Tullius (106-43 B.C)
 M. T. Cicero's Cato Major, or His Discourse of Old-Age: With Explanatory Notes [translated by James Logan]
 Philadelphia: B. Franklin, 1744 [first state]. H. 20 cm.
 Lent by The Houghton Library; bequest of Harriet J. Bradbury, 1930. AC7.L8284.744c

11 FEKE, Robert (ca. 1707-ca. 1752), American
 Benjamin Franklin, ca. 1746
 Oil on canvas. H. 127.5 x 102.5 cm.
 Ex coll.: John Franklin (ca. 1746-1756); Mrs. John Franklin (1756-1768); her son Tuthill Hubbart (1768-1814); his sister Elizabeth Hubbart Partridge (1808-1814); her niece Susan Hubbart Bean (1814-1828); her brother-in-law Thomas Waldron Sumner (1828-1849); Dr. John Collins Warren (1850-1856).
 Bibliography: Sellers, Benjamin Franklin in Portraiture, pp. 24-45 and 281, pl. 1.
  R. Peter Mooz, Philadelphia Painting and Printing, Exhibition Catalogue of the Pennsylvania Academy of the Fine Arts (Philadelphia: 1971), cat. no 10.
  Mooz, American Painting to 1776: A Reappraisal, Winterthur Conference Report, ed. I. M. G. Quimby (1971), p. 203.
 Harvard University Portrait Collection; bequest of Dr. John Collins Warren, 1856. H 47

12 [Franklin, Benjamin]
 Proposals Relating to the Education of Youth in Pensilvania.
 Philadelphia: [B. Franklin and D. Hall, 1749]. H. 17.5 cm.
 Lent by The Houghton Library; bequest of William Prescott, 1845.
 *AC7.F8545.749p

13 Franklin, Benjamin
 Experiments and Observations on Electricity, Made at Philadelphia in America . . .
 London: E. Cave, 1751-53. H. 21.5 cm.
 Lent by The Houghton Library; probably gift of the author before 1764. Phys 80.3.1*

14 COPLEY, John Singleton (1738-1815), American
John Winthrop (1714-1779), Hollis Professor of Mathematics and Natural Philosophy, 1773
Oil on canvas. H. 127.5 x 102.5 cm.
Bibliography: Huntsinger, *Harvard Portraits* . . ., pp. 149-51 (ill.).
Prown, *John Singleton Copley*, 1:89, 235, fig. 328.
Harvard University Portrait Collection; gift of the executors of the estate of John Winthrop of Rhode Island, grandson of Professor Winthrop, to Harvard College, 1894. H 113

15 SHORT, James (1710-1768), English
Reflecting Telescope, ca. 1740
Brass. Barrel: L. 30.5, Diam. 8.3 cm. Inscribed, on barrel: JAMES SHORT LONDON $\frac{163}{954}$ = 12
Bibliography: Wheatland, *The Apparatus* . . ., pp. 12-13.
Lent by the Collection of Historical Scientific Instruments; gift of the heirs of John Winthrop to Harvard College. No. 53
This portable telescope on a folding tripod is the one Copley painted in his portrait of Winthrop. It belonged to the professor, who kept it at home. Thus it escaped the fire of 1764, which consumed the apparatus collection in Harvard Hall.

16 Franklin, Benjamin
Autograph letter, signed, to James Bowdoin. Philadelphia, 12 April 1753.
Ink on paper. H. 20.5 x 16.5 cm.
Courtesy of The Massachusetts Historical Society.

17 COPLEY, John Singleton (1738-1815), American
Edward Holyoke (1689-1769), President of Harvard College, 1759-61
Oil on canvas. H. 128.5 x 103 cm.
Bibliography: Huntsinger, *Harvard Portraits* . . ., pp. 76-78 (ill.).
Prown, *John Singleton Copley*, 1:33-34 and 219; fig. 92.
Harvard University Portrait Collection; gift of Mrs. Turner and Mrs. Ward, granddaughters of President Holyoke, to Harvard College, 1829. H 6

18 Harvard College

Master of Arts Diploma conferred on Benjamin Franklin. 25 July 1753

Box: tin, painted blue-green, emblazoned with arms of Harvard College: on a red shield a brown (once silver?) chevron between three brown open books, with red and gold torse and scroll-work. H. 21 x 11 cm.; Diploma: Ink on parchment. H. 31.8 x 39.5 cm.

Bibliography: Lane, *Harvard College,* following pp. 230 and 238 (engraved ill. of diploma, seal and box);
Samuel Eliot Morison, "Harvard Seals and Arms," *The Harvard Graduates' Magazine* (Sept. 1933): 1-15.

Lent by The American Philosophical Society.

The seal was impressed with a die cast in 1693 by the famous Boston silversmith, John Coney. Professor Morison calls this "the most beautiful of all the Harvard seals."

19 Benjamin Franklin

Autograph letter, signed, to Thomas Hancock (1702/3-1764); with manuscript, signed subscription form; and autograph, signed draft for 4 pistoles. Philadelphia, 11 September 1755.

Ink on paper. Letter (folded, leaf): H. 33.3 x 21.3 cm.; subscription form (folded, leaf): H. 33 x 21 cm.; draft: H. 11 x 21 cm.

Lent by The Houghton Library.   fMS Am 1310

20 Franklin, Benjamin

Manuscript copy of a letter to Thomas Hubbard (d. 1773). London, 28 April 1758.

Ink on paper. H. 32.5 x 20.4 cm.
Lent by by The Houghton Library.   fMS Am 1310

21 Virgil (Publius Vergilius Maro, 70-19 B.C.)

Bucolica, Georgica, et Æneis

Birmingham: J. Baskerville, 1757.   H. 27 cm.
Lent by The Houghton Library; gift of Benjamin Franklin, 1758.
x17.09.2

This volume bears the first bookplate used by the College Library. It was engraved by Nathaniel Hurd to specifications voted by the Corporation in December, 1765. On this example is written: "The Gift of Benjamin Franklin/Recd 1758/ This book escaped the fire of Jan. 1764."

22 Mico, Joseph (d. 1772)
Autograph letter, signed, to Thomas Hubbard (d. 1773). London, 13 May 1758.

Ink on paper. H. 23 x 18.5 cm.
Lent by the Harvard University Archives.

23 Franklin, Benjamin
Autograph letter, signed, to John Winthrop (1714-1779). Philadelphia, 10 July 1764.

Ink on paper. Folded, leaf: H. 21.3 x 18.5 cm.
Lent by The Houghton Library; gift of John Winthrop, Newport, R. I., 1876. fMS Am 1310

24 SHORT, James (1710-1768), English
Reflecting Telescope with Finder, 1765-69

Brass. Barrel tube: L. 152, Diam. 20 cm. Inscribed, on eyepiece end of barrel: JAMES SHORT LONDON 9=48; below: 1817/REMOUNTED BY/W&S JONES/N 30 Holborn/London (W&S Jones made the wood and brass tripod in 1817).
Bibliography: Cohen, *Some Early Tools* . . ., pp. 154-55, fig. 1. Wheatland, *The Apparatus* . . ., pp. 17-19.
Lent by the Collection of Historical Scientific Instruments; gift of Thomas Hollis of Lincolns Inn, 1767. No. 1

25 BIRD, John (1709-1776), English
Meridian Telescope and Equal Altitudes Instrument, 1768

Brass (fitted to iron shaft and mahogany stand). Barrel: L. 99, Diam. 4 cm. Inscribed, on barrel: J.BIRD, LONDON.
Bibliography: Wheatland, *The Apparatus* . . ., pp. 38-39.
Lent by the Collection of Historical Scientific Instruments; gift of Thomas Hollis of Lincolns Inn, 1767. No. 58

NO. 22 Joseph Mico, Harvard's agent in London, submitted financial statements to the Treasurer of the College accompanied by letters like the one above. He never charged the College a commission for attending to its affairs in England, and after his death it was voted "That the Corporation have a grateful sense of these services, and must ever pay a particular respect to his memory."

TWO

LECTURES

ON THE

Parallax and Distance of the Sun,

AS DEDUCIBLE FROM

The Tranſit of Venus.

Read in Holden-Chapel at HARVARD-COLLEGE in Cambridge, *New-England*, in March 1769.

By JOHN WINTHROP, Esq.

Hollisian Profeſſor of the Mathematics and Philoſophy at *Cambridge*, and F. R. S.

Agite, mortales! et oculos in Spectaculum vertite, quod hucuſque ſpectaverunt perpauciſſimi; ſpectaturi iterum ſunt nulli.

Publiſhed by the general Deſire of the Students.

B O S T O N:
PRINTED AND SOLD BY EDES & GILL IN QUEEN-STREET,
M,DCC,LXIX.

26 Winthrop, John (1714-1779)
Two Lectures on the Parallax and Distance of the Sun, as Deducible from the Transit of Venus.
Boston: Edes & Gill, 1769. H. 19 cm.
Lent by the Harvard University Archives. HUC 8769.295

Dear Sir, London, March 11. 1769

At length after much Delay & Difficulty I have been able to obtain your Telescope, that was made by Mr Short before his Death. His Brother, who succeeds in the Business, has setted it up and compleated it. He has followed the Business many Years at Edinburgh, is reckon'd very able, and therefore I hope every thing will be found right; but as it is only just finish'd, I have no time left to get any philosophical or astronomical Friends to examine it as I intended, the Ship being on the Point of sailing, and a future Opportunity uncertain. Enclos'd is his Direction Paper for opening & fixing it. — I have not yet got the Bill of the Price: it is to be made from the deceased Mr Short's Book of Memorandums of Orders, in which he enter'd this Order of ours as it is suppos'd the Price: I do not remember, it is so long since, whether it was 100 £ or 100 Guineas. and the Book is in the Hands of the Executors, as I understand — When I have the Account I shall pay it as I did Bird's for the Transit Instrument, which 40 Guineas, and then shall apply for the whole to Mr Mauduit. — By the way, I wonder that I have not heard from you of the Receipt of that Instrument, which went from hence in September by Capt Watt. I hope it got safe to hand, and gave Satisfaction. The Ship was the same that Mr Rogers went in, who I hear arriv'd

John Winthrop Esqr

arived, and by him too I sent the Philosophic Transactions, with a Number of Copies of your Paper as printed Separately. But I have no Letter from you since that by the young Gentleman you recommended to me, Grandson to Sir W[m] Pepperell, which I think was dated about the Beginning of October, when you could not have receiv'd them.

By a late Ship, I sent your College a Copy of the new Edition of my Philosophical Papers, and others I think for yourself & for M[r] Bowdoin. I should apologize to you for inserting therein some part of our Correspondence without first obtaining your Permission; But as M[r] Bowdoin had favour'd me with his Consent, for what related to him, I ventur'd to rely on your Good Nature as to what related to you, and I hope you will forgive me.

I have got from M[r] Ellicot the Glasses of the long Galilean Telescope which he presents to your College. I put them into the Hands of M[r] Nairne, the Optician, to examine & put them in Order. I thought to have sent them by this Ship, but am disappointed; they shall go by the next if possible.

There is nothing new here in the philosophical Way at present.

With great and sincere Esteem, I am,
Dear Sir,
    Your most obedient &
    most humble Servant,
        B Franklin

P.S. There is no Prospect of getting the Duty &c. repeal'd this Session of Parl. Your Non Importation Resolutions to consume no more British goods may possibly if persisted in have a good Effect another Year. I apprehend the Parliamentary Resolves & Address will tend to widen the Breach. Inclos'd I send you Gov[r] Pownall's Speech against those Resolves; his Name is not to be mention'd. He appears to me a hearty Friend to America; tho' I find he is suspected by some on account of his Connections.

27 Franklin, Benjamin
Autograph letter, signed, to John Winthrop, London, 11 March 1769.
Ink on paper. H. 32.5 x 20.5 cm.
Lent by The American Philosophical Society.

28 Martin, Benjamin (1704-1782)
The Young Gentleman and Lady's Philosophy . . ., Vol. I
London: W. Owen, 1759. H. 21 cm.
Lent by The Houghton Library; gift of David P. Wheatland, 1973.
*EC75.M3632.755ga, pt. 1, vol. 1 (A)

NO. 28

29 MARTIN, Benjamin (1704-1782), English
Weights and Pulleys, ca. 1765

Brass; mahogany frame. H. 82.8, L. 55, W. 39.5 cm. Inscribed, on double block: B. Martin London
Bibliography: Cohen, *Some Early Tools* . . ., p. 158, fig. 8.
Wheatland, *The Apparatus* . . ., pp. 86-87.

Lent by the Collection of Historical Scientific Instruments. No. 8

30 MARTIN, Benjamin (1704-1782), English, attributed to.
Electrostatic Machine, ca. 1766

Mahogany frame, brass conductors, glass sphere, leather cushion. H. 189, L. 182, W. 69 cm. Diam. of wheel 122 cm.
Bibliography: Cohen, Some Early Tools . . ., pp. 159-60, fig. 12.
Wheatland, The Apparatus . . ., pp. 136-37.
Lent by the Collection of Historical Scientific Instruments. No. 12
When the glass globe of this machine was whirled against the leather "rubber," it generated an electric charge which was received by the brass rods through the small chains which dangled from them. The charge taken from the rods was stored in a Leyden jar.

31 Winthrop, John (1714-1779)
Holograph notebook: *Summary of a Course of Experimental Philosophical Lectures*

Cambridge, Massachusetts [1746]. Ink on paper, bound in brown leather. H. 15 cm.
Lent by the Harvard College Archives; gift of Robert C. Winthrop, 1869. HUC 8745.294

32 MARTIN, Benjamin (1704-1782), English
Orrery with Clockwork Mechanism, 1765-66

Brass; silvered brass concentric rings; ivory earth. H. 77 cm.; Diam. of drum 56.3 cm. Inscribed, on top edge of drum: Made & Improv'd/by B. MARTIN in/Fleet Street LONDON./The Gift of the/Honble. JAMES BOWDOIN ESQ./To the Apparatus of Harvard College/N.E. May 1764; on ecliptic circle: calendar and zodiac; on meridian circles: scales
Bibliography: Cohen, Some Early Tools . . ., pp. 156-57, fig. 4.
Wheatland, The Apparatus . . ., pp. 52-53.
Lent by the Collection of Historical Scientific Instruments; gift of James Bowdoin, 1764. No. 4

33 WILTON, Joseph (1722-1803), English
William Pitt, Earl of Chatham (1708-1778), ca. 1759

Plaster. H. 57 x 48 cm. Inscribed, on back: WM. PITT./EARL CHATHAM

Bibliography: H. W. White, "Nineteenth-Century American Sculpture at Harvard," *Harvard Library Bulletin,* Vol. XVIII, no. 4 (Oct. 1970), 359, pl. II.

Harvard University Portrait Collection; gift of Benjamin Franklin to Harvard College, 1769. P 17

34 Franklin, Benjamin
Experiments and Observations on Electricity, Made at Philadelphia in America. . . . To Which Are Added, Letters and Papers on Philosophical Subjects . . .

London: D. Henry, 1769. H. 23 cm.

Lent by The Houghton Library; gift of Thomas Hollis, 1769. Phys 80.3*

35 Maseres, Francis (1731-1824)
Elements of Plane Trigonometry . . . and the Nature and Use of Logarithms

London: T. Parker, 1760. H. 20 cm.

Lent by The Houghton Library; gift of Benjamin Franklin. x17-09.4*

36 FISHER, Edward (1730-1785), English, after Mason Chamberlin (d. 1787), English
Benjamin Franklin

Mezzotint (second state); plate retouched with burin. Cut to plate mark: H. 37.6 x 27.5 cm. Inscribed, below design area, l.l.: M: Chamberlin pinx.; l.r.: E. Fisher fecit.; l.c.: B. Franklin of Philadelphia L.L.D. F.R.S./Sold by M..Chamberlin in Stewart Street, Old Artillery Ground, Spittalfields, — Price 5".

Ex. coll.: Harvard College Archives (June 24, 1771-February 18, 1944)

Bibliography: Sellers, *Benjamin Franklin in Portraiture,* pp. 57-60, 220-21.

Fogg Art Museum, Print Department; gift of Benjamin Franklin, 1771. M 10,977

37 Priestley, Joseph (1733-1804)
 The History and Present State of Electricity . . .
 London: J. Dodsley et al., 1767. H. 26.5 cm.
 Lent by The Houghton Library; gift of Benjamin Franklin, 1772.
 AC7.F8545.Zz767p

38 Vattel, Emmerich de (1714-1767)
 Le Droit des Gens, ou, Principes de la Loi Naturelle . . .
 Amsterdam: E. van Harrevelt, 1775. H. 26.5 cm.
 Lent by The Houghton Library; gift of the editor, Charles Guillaume Frédéric Dumas, through Benjamin Franklin, 1776.
 x17.09.6*

39 Continental Congress of the United States
 Appointment and instructions to commissioners Benjamin Franklin, Silas Deane and Thomas Jefferson, signed by John Hancock, President, and attested by Chas. Thomson. Philadelphia, 30 September 1776.
 Ink on paper. H. 40.5 x 32 cm.
 Lent by The Houghton Library; gift of Richard H. Lee, 1827.
 bMS Am 811.1 (73)
 Thomas Jefferson was unable to serve. A copy of this commission, also at The Houghton Library, substitutes the name of "Arthur Lee of the State of Virginia" for "Thomas Jefferson a delegate from the state of Virginia" — an unfortunate exchange from Franklin's viewpoint.

40 NINI, Jean-Baptiste (1717-1786), French
 Medallion profile of Benjamin Franklin
 Terra cotta. Diam. 11.8 cm. Signed, impressed on *tranche* of shoulder: NINI/F 1777; in relief, arms; and below, 1777. Inscribed, within self-frame border: .B.FRANKLIN. .AMERICAIN.
 Mark, stamped on reverse: small fleur-de-lis
 Bibliography: Storelli, *Jean-Baptiste Nini* . . ., no. LXI.
 Sellers, *Benjamin Franklin in Portraiture*, pp. 343-45, pl. 10.
 Gift of Grenville L. Winthrop. 1938.33

41 SAINT AUBIN, Augustin de (1736-1807), French, after Charles Nicolas Cochin, the younger (1715-1790), French

Benjamin Franklin

Etching and engraving. Plate mark: H. 20.4 x 14.9 cm. Inscribed, within the design area, center: BENJAMIN FRANKLIN./Né à Boston, dans la nouvelle Angleterre le 17.Janvier 1706.; l.l.: C. N. Cochin fecit et delin. 1777; l.r.: Aug. de St. Aubin sculp. Inscribed, center, below design area: Dessiné par C. N. Cochin Chevalier de l'Ordre du Roi, en 1777 et Gravé par Aug. de St. Aubin, Graveur de la Bibliothèque du Roi/Se vend à Paris chez C. N. Cochin aux Galleries du Louvre, et chez Aug. de St. Aubin, rue des Mathurins.

Bibliography: Sellers, *Benjamin Franklin in Portraiture,* pp. 96-99, 108-09, 227-30.

Gift of John Witt Randall. R 4409

42 NINI, Jean-Baptiste (1717-1786), French

Medallion profile of Benjamin Franklin

Terra cotta. Diam. 9 cm. Signed, impressed on *tranche* of shoulder: NINI F; in relief, arms

Bibliography: Storelli, *Jean-Baptiste Nini* . . ., no. LXIV.
Sellers, *Benjamin Franklin in Portraiture,* pp. 343-46, pl. 10.

Gift of Grenville L. Winthrop. 1938.35

43 NINI, Jean-Baptiste (1717-1786), French

Medallion profile of Benjamin Franklin

Terra cotta. Oval: H. 15.2 x 15.7 cm. Signed, impressed on *tranche* of bust: I.B. NINI. F./1778.; in relief, on *tranche* of shoulder, arms; and below, NINI F 1779. Inscribed, around edge: ERIPUIT·COELO·FULMEN·SCEPTRUMQUE·TIRANNIS·

Bibliography: Storelli, *Jean-Baptiste Nini* . . ., cf. no. LXVIII.
Sellers, *Benjamin Franklin in Portraiture,* pp. 347-48, pl. 11 (this example, but caption is reversed with that of medallion on its right).

Gift of Grenville L. Winthrop. 1938.37

44 DUPLESSIS, Joseph-Siffred (1725-1802), French (Replica by the artist of the portrait signed and dated 1778.)

Benjamin Franklin

Oil on canvas. Oval: H. 72 x 59 cm.
Ex coll.: The Earl of Rosebery (1847-1929)
Bibliography: Sellers, "Collectors Notes," *Antiques,* Vol. 52; no. 2 (Aug. 1957): 156 (ill.).
Sellers, *Benjamin Franklin in Portraiture,* pp. 246ff., 260, no. 19.
Bequest of Grenville L. Winthrop. 1943.235

45 CHEVILLET, Juste (1729-1802), French, after Joseph-Siffred Duplessis (1725-1802), French
Benjamin Franklin
Engraving. Plate mark: H. 30.7 x 20.6 cm. Inscribed, below design area, l.l.: Duplessis Pinxit Parisiis 1778.; l.r.: Chevillet Sculpsit.; center: Tiré du Cabinet de M. Le Ray de Chaumont &ca. Inscribed, within design area: BENJAMIN FRANKLIN/Né à Boston, dans la nouvelle Angleterre, le 17 Janv. 1706./Below, a four-line laudatory verse by M. Feutry.
Bibliography: Sellers, *Benjamin Franklin in Portraiture,* pp. 133-34, 249.
Gift of Mrs. Williams Simes. M 9385

46 CAFFIÉRI, Jean Jacques (1725-1792), French (copy, by an unidentified Italian sculptor, derived from terra-cotta bust modelled in 1777)
Benjamin Franklin, bust
Marble. H. 54 x 51 cm.
Bibliography: Sellers, *Benjamin Franklin in Portraiture,* pp. 197ff.
Gift of Howland Warren, Richard Warren, and Mary Warren Murphy. 1961.27

47 HOUDON, Jean Antoine (1741-1828), French (copy, derived from terra-cotta bust modelled in 1778)
Benjamin Franklin, bust
Bronze. H. 35 x 30 cm. Signed, on edge of right shoulder: houdon *f.* 1778
Bibliography: Sellers, *Benjamin Franklin in Portraiture,* pp. 304ff.
Bequest of Grenville L. Winthrop. 1943.1269

48 French, Sèvres, 18th century (possibly by Josse François Joseph Leriche [1738-1812], derived from terra-cotta bust modelled by Caffiéri in 1777)

Benjamin Franklin, bust
Soft paste porcelain, unglazed. H. 23.5 x 21.3 cm. Inscribed, incised on back: L R / 3
Bibliography: Sellers, Benjamin Franklin in Portraiture, pp. 371-72, pl. 14 (this example).
Bequest of Grenville L. Winthrop. 1943.1163

49 French, 18th century (derived from terra-cotta bust modelled by Caffiéri in 1777)
Benjamin Franklin, bust
Bust: silver, gilded. H. 11.7 x 12 cm. Pedestal: crystal, with gilt bronze mounts, H. 17.7, Diam. 13.7 cm.
Bequest of Grenville L. Winthrop. 1943.1074

50 SUZANNE, François Marie (ca. 1750-1802), French (derived from terra cotta modelled in 1793)
Benjamin Franklin, statuette
Plaster. H., including integral base, 42 cm.
Bibliography: Sellers, Benjamin Franklin in Portraiture, pp. 373-74.
Bequest of Grenville L. Winthrop. 1943.1681

51 English, Staffordshire (ca. 1800)
Benjamin Franklin
Earthenware, glazed. H. 39.4 x 16 cm. Inscribed, on base: General Washington
Lent by the Rose Art Museum; gift of Mr. and Mrs. Edward Rose. 1961.284

52 French, 18th century (derived from an engraving by "N.L.G.D.L.C.A.D.L.," 1780, after a portrait by Anne Rosalie Filleul (1752-1794), French
Benjamin Franklin, miniature
Oil on tortoiseshell. Oval: H. 9 x 6.6 cm.
Bibliography: Sellers, Benjamin Franklin in Portraiture, pp. 281-84.
Bequest of Grenville L. Winthrop. 1943.1631

53 French, Unidentified artist: "N.L.G.D.L.C.A.D.L."
Benjamin Franklin: Oval Portrait Held by Diogenes, 1780
Engraving. Cut, within plate mark: H. 32.3 x 21 cm. Inscribed, below design area: N.L.G.D.L.C.A.D.L. del. et sculp./ BENJAMIN FRANKLIN/Ministre plenipotentiaire a la Cour de France pour la Republique/des Provinces unies de l'Amerique Septentrionale./Né à Boston le 17, Janvier 1706./A Paris chez Bligny Lancier du Roi, Md. d'Estampes, Peintre, Doreur et Vitrier, Cour du Manège aux Thuilleries. Added to right of above inscription: Presenté à son Excellence/quelle à acceptée le 14./Juillet 1780./ Par son très Humble et très Obéissant/Serviteur BLIGNY. Inscribed, within design area, on stone at Diogenes's feet: STUPETE GENTES! REPERIT VIVUM DIOGENES; on map: AMERIQ. SEPTENT.
Bibliography: Sellers, Benjamin Franklin in Portraiture, pp. 283-84.
Courtesy of Boston Public Library, Print Department.

"Heads of Illustrious Moderns"

Josiah Wedgwood perfected the jasper body so suitable for portrait medallions in 1775. These enjoyed great popularity, and by 1788 Wedgwood listed in his catalogue nearly 1700 portrait cameos and medallions. The finest among these portrayed his eminent contemporaries, who were included in Class X of the catalogue: "Heads of Illustrious Moderns from Chaucer to the Present Time."

54 Benjamin Franklin
Probably modelled by William Hackwood (d. 1836) after Jean-Baptiste Nini
Blue and white jasper. H. 6.4 x 5.1 cm. Impressed, below *tranche*: Dr. FRANKLIN.
Mark: Wedgwood/& Bentley. 1778
Bibliography: Reilly and Savage, Wedgwood . . ., p. 145 (ill. *on left*).
Sellers, Benjamin Franklin in Portraiture, p. 397, pl. 10.
Bequest of Grenville L. Winthrop. 1943.1217

55 Charlotte Sophia (1744-1818)
Queen Consort of George III, and mother of their fifteen children.
Possibly modelled by Henry Burch (1730-1814)
Lavender-pink and white jasper. H. 9 x 6.8 cm. (sight).
Mark: WEDGWOOD ca. 1789
Ex coll.: King George III; Queen Victoria; J. Rouston; Arthur Sanderson
Bibliography: Reilly and Savage, *Wedgwood* . . ., p. 98, pl. VII (this example, in color).
Bequest of Grenville L. Winthrop. 1943.1210

56 George III, King of England (1738-1820)

Modelled by Henry Burch (1730-1814)

Lavender-pink and white jasper. H. 9 x 6.8 cm. (sight).
Mark: WEDGWOOD   ca. 1789

Ex coll.: King George III; Queen Victoria; J. Rouston; Arthur Sanderson

Bibliography: Reilly and Savage, *Wedgwood* . . ., p. 166, pl. VII (this example, in color).

Bequest of Grenville L. Winthrop.   1943.1220

57 Doctor Joseph Priestley (1733-1804)

Intimate friend and colleague of Wedgwood and Franklin. Wedgwood assisted him financially and manufactured for him specially designed chemical apparatus. In 1779 Wedgwood wrote to his partner, Bentley, "Dr. Priestley is arriv'd & we are with great reverence taking off his presbyterian parson's wig & preparing a Sr I. Newton as a companion to him."

Modelled by Giuseppe Cerracchi (1751-1802)

Blue and white jasper. H. 27.9 x 20.3 cm.
Mark: WEDGWOOD/& BENTLEY   1779

Ex coll.: Dr. Joseph Priestley (at his Pennsylvania residence 1794-1804); Dr. J. Lumsden Propert

Bibliography: Reilly and Savage, Wedgwood . . ., p. 284 (ill., this example)

Jean Gorely and Marvin D. Schwartz, *The Emily Winthrop Miles Collection* (New York: The Brooklyn Museum, 1965), p. 37, no. 4.

Frederick Rathbone, *Catalogue of the Wedgwood Museum* (Stoke-on-Trent, 1909), no. 110.

Lent by The Brooklyn Museum; The Emily Winthrop Miles Collection. 57.180.2

NO. 58   NO. 59

58 Granville Leveson-Gower, Earl Gower, Marquis of Stafford (1721-1803)

Friend and patron of Wedgwood, he guided through Parliament the legislation that permitted the construction of the Trent and Mersey canal. He was President of the Privy Council in 1774 when Wedderburn delivered his slanderous attack on Benjamin Franklin. In 1779, unable to endure their Lordships' obtuseness any longer, he resigned the office.

Blue and white jasper. H. 8.7 x 6.8 cm. Scratched on back: new 3601
Mark: WEDGWOOD/" ca. 1788
Ex coll.: E. B. Holden
Bibliography: Reilly and Savage, Wedgwood . . ., p. 313.
Bequest of Grenville L. Winthrop. 1943.1379

59 Sir William Hamilton (1730-1803)

For thirty-six years English ambassador to Naples, he participated in the excavations at Pompeii and Herculaneum, and promoted the neoclassic style through his collection and publication of Greek and Roman antiquities. He purchased from the Barberini family the "Portland Vase" from which Wedgwood made his famous copies.

Pink and white jasper. H. 10.4 x 8.2 cm. (sight). Impressed, below tranche: s. w. HAMILTON.
Mark: WEDGWOOD ca. 1787
Bibliography: Reilly and Savage, Wedgwood . . ., p. 182
Bequest of Grenville L. Winthrop. 1943.1201

60 William Eden, Lord Auckland (1744-1814)

On December 31, 1777, one of Eden's spies wrote him "Dr. Franklin is a life — and does nothing but fly from one part of Paris to t'other" (Letters . . ., ed. Smyth, 10:329). Four months later Eden was en route to America as commissioner for Restoring Peace.

Modelled by Eley George Mountstephen (fl. 1781-1791)
Blue and white jasper. H. 11 x 8.7 cm.
Mark: WEDGWOOD ca. 1790
Bibliography: Reilly and Savage, Wedgwood . . ., p. 52
Bequest of Grenville L. Winthrop. 1943.1211

NO. 60

NO. 61

NO. 62

NO. 63

61 Lady Auckland (1758-1818)

Modelled by Eley George Mountstephen (fl. 1781-1791)
Blue and white jasper. H. 11 x 8.7 cm.
Mark: WEDGWOOD   ca. 1790
Bibliography: Reilly and Savage, *Wedgwood* . . ., p. 52
Bequest of Grenville L. Winthrop. 1943.1212

62 William Pitt (1759-1806)

Still a youth when Franklin visited his father, the Earl of Chatham, young Pitt nevertheless listened to their discussions and later helped his father prepare speeches in defense of the Colonies' rights. He had had a thorough political education by the time he became Prime Minister at the age of twenty-three.

Blue and white jasper. H. 9.2 x 7.3 cm.
Mark: WEDGWOOD   ca. 1787
Bibliography: Reilly and Savage, *Wedgwood* . . ., p. 276
Bequest of Grenville L. Winthrop. 1943.1202

63 Thomas Pitt, First Baron Camelford (1737-1793)

Cousin of William Pitt, he spoke in Parliament on Franklin's behalf during the peace negotiations.

Light purple and white jasper. H. 8.4 x 6.5 cm. Inscribed, on back:
    Gron in a dish/Light purple/the Body/mixt 300 to 1/NO 3919
Mark: WEDGWOOD   ca. 1787
Bibliography: Reilly and Savage, *Wedgwood* . . ., p. 82
Bequest of Grenville L. Winthrop. 1943.1191

64 Charles Pratt, First Earl Camden (1713-1794)

Lord High Commissioner from 1766 to 1770, he and William Pitt led the attack in Parliament against the oppressive measures so offensive to Americans. Franklin "was charm'd with his generous and noble Sentiments" (*Letters* . . ., ed. Smyth, 6:351).

Modelled after a medal by Thomas Pingo

Blue and white jasper. H. 4.3 x 3.5 cm. (sight).
Trial marks: B 1 & 1/2 & 1
Bibliography: Reilly and Savage, *Wedgwood* . . ., p. 81.
    Scheidemantel, "Josiah Wedgwood's . . ., 3:17, no. 85.
Bequest of Grenville L. Winthrop. 1943.1207

NO. 64   NO. 65

65 Mrs. Elizabeth Montagu (1720-1800)

Author of many essays and letters, she entertained the intelligentsia of both sexes at her salon, which was mockingly referred to as the Blue Stocking Society.

Lavender and white jasper. H. 4.3 x 3.2 cm.
Mark: WEDGWOOD   ca. 1775
Bibliography: Reilly and Savage, *Wedgwood* . . ., p. 246.
Bequest of Grenville L. Winthrop. 1943.1609

66 Viscount Richard Howe (1726-1799)

An admirer of Franklin, he tried to negotiate a settlement for the Colonies before Franklin left for Philadelphia in 1775. He came to America in the summer of 1776 as both Commander-in-Chief of the British Navy and as Peace Commissioner, but his terms offered too little too late.

Modelled by John de Vaere (b. 1755)
Lavender and white jasper. H. 9.6 x 7.4 cm. (sight).
Mark: WEDGWOOD   ca. 1798
Bibliography: Reilly and Savage, *Wedgwood* . . ., p. 195.
Bequest of Grenville L. Winthrop. 1943.1195

NO. 66   NO. 68

67 Sir Joseph Banks (1743-1820)

   A distinguished naturalist and explorer, he was President of the Royal Society from 1778 until his death. Franklin sent him detailed accounts of the balloon ascents which created a sensation in postwar Paris.

   Modelled by John Flaxman (1755-1826), 1775
   Blue and white jasper. H. 8 x 6.3 cm. (sight).
   Ex coll.: William Erasmus Darwin
   Mark: WEDGWOOD/& BENTLEY   ca. 1776
   Bibliography: Reilly and Savage, *Wedgwood* . . ., p. 55.
   Bequest of Grenville L. Winthrop. 1943.1199

68 Dr. John Fothergill (1712-1780)

   The Quaker physician who had written the preface to the first edition of *Experiments and Observations on Electrictiy* . . ., he became one of Franklin's closest friends after his arrival in London in 1757.

   Modelled by John Flaxman (1755-1826)
   Green and white jasper. H. 9.7 x 7.7 cm. Impressed, below *tranche:* FOTHERGILL
   Mark: WEDGWOOD   ca. 1785
   Bibliography: Reilly and Savage, *Wedgwood* . . ., p. 143.
   Bequest of Grenville L. Winthrop. 1943.1194

69 Sir William Herschel (1738-1822)

German-born musician and astronomer, he discovered the planet Uranus in 1781.

Modelled by John Flaxman (1755-1826), 1783
Green and white jasper. H. 12.5 x 10 cm. Impressed, below *tranche:* HERSCHEL
Mark: WEDGWOOD ca. 1783
Ex coll.: W. D. Holt
Bibliography: Reilly and Savage, *Wedgwood* . . ., pp. 191-92 (variation of this example).
Bequest of Grenville L. Winthrop. 1943.1239

70 Benjamin West (1738-1820)

As a young man, he left Philadelphia for London carrying letters of introduction from Benjamin Franklin. There he became a successful painter and President of the Royal Academy. He painted Franklin among the commissioners in "The Treaty of Paris" in 1784-5, and many years later the romantic tribute "Franklin Drawing Electricity from the Sky."

Blue and white jasper. H. 10.6 x 8.4 cm. Impressed, below *tranche:* WEST
Mark: WEDGWOOD 1785-1790
Bibliography: Reilly and Savage, *Wedgwood* . . ., p. 337.
Bequest of Grenville L. Winthrop. 1943.1193

71 David Garrick (1717-1779)

Distinguished actor, and partner in the Drury Lane Theatre, he arranged "a benefit for the colleges of Philadelphia and New York" at the Theatre on April 27, 1763. (George Winchester Stone, ed., *The London Stage, 1660-1800*, Vol. 5, Carbondale: Southern Illinois Press [1968]).

Modelled by William Hackwood (d. 1836), 1777
Black basalt in pendant sunburst frame. H. 5.3 x 4.5 cm. Impressed, below *tranche:* GARRICK.
Mark: WEDGWOOD/& BENTLEY ca. 1779
Bibliography: Reilly and Savage, *Wedgwood* . . ., p. 159.
Bequest of Grenville L. Winthrop. 1943.1273

THE CATALOGUE 135

NO. 69

NO. 70

NO. 71

Two of Franklin's Scottish friends are represented here — in the company of an Irish ally — on medallions modelled by their compatriots, James and William Tassie.

72 James Tassie (1735-1799)

While working as a stonemason in Glasgow, he became interested in drawing and modelling. With Dr. Henry Quin he invented a glass paste for imitating engraved gems. The same material served to cast the portrait medallions he modelled. The competition with Wedgwood was amicable, Tassie sometimes supplying him with portraits for reproduction in jasper.

Modelled by William Tassie (1777-1860), his nephew

White and transparent glass on black backing. H. 10.6 x 6.6 cm. (sight). Signed, on *tranche* of bust: *W. Tassie F.* 1799. Inscribed, on *tranche* of shoulder: JAMES TASSIE/ DIED/JUNE 1799/IN HIS 64 YEAR

Bibliography: Gray, *James and William Tassie,* no. 379, pl. IX.

Bequest of Grenville L. Winthrop.   1943.1100

NO. 72   NO. 73

73 John Tassie (b. 1740)

Younger brother and assistant of James Tassie.

Modelled by James Tassie, 1791

White glass. H. 9.3 x 6.9 cm. Signed, on *tranche* of bust: *Tassie F.* Inscribed, on *tranche* of shoulder: JOHN TASSIE/1791

Ex coll.: Tassie family

Bibliography: Gray, *James and William Tassie*, no. 381.

Bequest of Grenville L. Winthrop. 1943.1101

74 Edmund Burke (1729-1797)

Born in Ireland, he was a vocal member of the opposition in Parliament, and a close friend of Benjamin Franklin. In 1766, while secretary to the Prime Minister, Lord Rockingham, he arranged for Franklin to appear for questioning before the House of Commons. Franklin's prepared answers convinced Parliament to repeal the Stamp Act.

NO. 74

Modelled by William Tassie (1777-1860) in 1797, after John Charles Lochée (b. 1751)

White glass. H. 10 x 7.1 cm. Signed and inscribed, on *tranche* of shoulder: EDMUND BURKE/W. Tassie F./1797

Ex coll.: Tassie family

Bibliography: Gray, *James and William Tassie*, no. 54.

Bequest of Grenville L. Winthrop.   1943.1090

75 Adam Smith (1723-1790)

Scottish economist and author of *The Wealth of Nations* (1776), he was influenced by Franklin's essay on population (1751). The two demographers became friends in 1759 at a party in Edinburgh honoring Franklin, who had come to Scotland to receive an honorary degree from the University of Saint Andrews.

Modelled by James Tassie, 1787

White glass. H. 9.5 x 6.9 cm. Signed, on *tranche* of bust: Tassie F. Inscribed, on *tranche* of shoulder: ADAM SMITH/IN HIS 64 YEAR/1787

Ex coll.: Tassie family

Bibliography: Gray, *James and William Tassie*, no. 356, pl. V.

Bequest of Grenville L. Winthrop.   1943.1099

NO. 75   NO. 76

76 David Hume (1711-1776)

Scottish historian and philosopher, Hume met Franklin during his visit to Scotland in 1759. When Franklin returned to Philadelphia in 1762, Hume wrote him, "America has sent us many good things . . . but you are the first philosopher and indeed the first great man of letters for whom we are beholden to her" (*Papers* . . ., ed. Labaree, 10:80).

Modelled by James Tassie, ca. 1775
White glass. H. 9.5 x 7.2 cm. Signed and inscribed, on *tranche* of shoulder: DAVID HUME/T.

Ex coll.: Tassie family

Bibliography: Gray, *James and William Tassie*, no. 198, pl. XIV.

Bequest of Grenville L. Winthrop. 1943.1096

77 Hume, David (1711-1776)

Autograph letter, signed, to Benjamin Franklin, Edinburgh, 7 February 1772.
Ink on paper. H. 22.8 x 19 cm.

Lent by The Houghton Library; from the Sparks Papers, collected by Jared Sparks. bMS Sparks 49.3 (198)

78 Franklin, Benjamin

Autograph letter, signed, to Arthur Lee (1740-1792), Passy, 1 February 1778.
Ink on paper. H. 23.5 x 19 cm.

Lent by The Houghton Library; gift of Richard H. Lee, 1827. bMS Am 811.3 (28a)

79 Jay, John (1745-1829)

Manuscript letter in the hand of an amanuensis, signed by Jay, to Benjamin Franklin, Philadelphia, June 1779.
Ink on paper. H. 32 x 20 cm.

Lent by The Houghton Library; from the Sparks Papers, collected by Jared Sparks. bMS Sparks 49.3 (56)

80 PEALE, Charles Willson (1741-1825), American

George Washington (1732-1799), 1784
Oil on canvas. H. 244 x 152 cm. Inscribed, l.l.: WASHINGTON

Ex coll.: probably descended in the families of Madame de Tessé, and of her brother, the Vicomte de Noailles, to his great-grandson, the Duc de Mouchy; Jonce I. McGurk, New York City (1930?-1942); [Martin Birnbaum].
Bibliography: Sellers, Portraits and Miniatures . . ., pp. 236-37, no. 936; p. 360 (ill.).
Bequest of Grenville L. Winthrop. 1943.144

On July 1, 1784, Governor Benjamin Harrison wrote to Peale to say that the Virginia Assembly had voted to erect a statue of Washington, and to ask the painter to complete immediately a full-length portrait of the General, to be shipped as soon as dry to Thomas Jefferson in France. Jefferson and Franklin, meanwhile, had been asked to get the painting to the best sculptor available. This, clearly, was Houdon, who insisted he could do a statue worthy of the great General only from life. He embarked for America in July, 1784, aboard the same ship as Franklin. But Peale had already dispatched his painting, a modified replica of that commissioned for the Annapolis House of Delegates, showing Washington at Yorktown, with the Articles of Capitulation on a table, and in the background the British colors cased between the French and American flags displayed. Apparently the portrait remained with Jefferson until he returned to America, when he gave it to Mme. de Tessé, sister of the Vicomte de Noailles, who, with his brother-in-law Lafayette, had led the French at Yorktown.

81 DUPRÉ, Augustin (1748-1833), French
Medal Honoring Benjamin Franklin, 1784

Brass; mother of pearl frame with ormolu mounts. Diam. 4.5 cm. Obverse: profile to left. Signed, on *tranche* of shoulder: DUPRÉ.F. Inscribed, around edge: BENJ. FRANKLIN NATUS BOSTON.XVII JAN./MDCCVI. Reverse: Genius of Liberty. Signed, in exergue: SCULPSIT ET DICAVIT/AUG. DUPRÉ ANNO/MDCCLXXXIV. Inscribed, around edge: ERIPUIT COELO FULMEN SCEPTRUM QUE TYRANNIS.
Bibliography: Sellers, Benjamin Franklin in Portraiture, p. 277, pl. 20.
Bequest of Grenville L. Winthrop. 1943.1625

82 COPLEY, John Singleton (1738-1815), American
John Adams (1735-1826), 1783

Oil on canvas. H. 238 x 147 cm.

Ex coll.: John Singleton Copley (1783-1815); Mrs. Copley (1815-17); John Adams (1817-18); lent to his cousin, Ward Nicholas Boylston (1818-28).

Bibliography: Andrew Oliver, Portraits of John and Abigail Adams (Cambridge: Harvard University Press, 1967), pp. 23-38, fig. 9.
Prown, John Singleton Copley, 2:300, 411; fig. 438.

Harvard University Portrait Collection; bequest of Ward Nicholas Boylston, 1828. H 74

83 Franklin, Benjamin
Pressed copy of autograph letter, signed, to Sir Joseph Banks (1743-1820), Passy, 21 November 1783.

Ink on paper. Five leaves; each, folded. H. 24.5 x 20.5 cm. (irregular).

Lent by The Houghton Library; gift in memory of Professor and Mrs. A. L. Rotch, 1942. fMS Am 1310.1

This is the first of a series of long letters to the President of the Royal Society detailing Montgolfier's balloon ascents. As Franklin wished copies for other scientific colleagues, he wrote with an ink which would be absorbed into transparent paper which was laid over it and subjected to great pressure.

84 GULLAGER, Christian (1759-1826), American
James Bowdoin II (1726-80), ca. 1791.

Oil on panel. H. 27.3 x 22 cm.

Bibliography: Louisa Dresser, "Christian Gullager, an Introduction to His Life and Some Representative Examples of His Work," Art in America, 37 (July, 1949): 103-79.
Marvin S. Sadik, Colonial and Federal Portraits at Bowdoin College (Bowdoin College Museum of Art, 1966), pp. 88-102.

Lent by Bowdoin College; gift of Miss Clara Bowdoin Winthrop, 1924.

Gullager, a painter of Danish birth and training who came to

Boston about 1787, has here shown the late Governor Bowdoin in his "Great Upper Chamber." An inventory of this room, made in 1774, listed over twelve hundred books, "an Electrical Machine and Apparatus," six telescopes and numerous other scientific instruments. Gullager may have based the likeness on a silhouette recently engraved by Samuel Hill, or on a miniature from which the engraving was said to be taken.

85 English, Wedgwood
   The Slave in Chains

   Modelled by William Hackwood (d. 1836)
   Black relief on white jasper. H. 3.5 x 2.8 cm. Inscribed, in relief around edge: AM I NOT A MAN AND A BROTHER.
   Mark, impressed twice, crossed: WEDGWOOD   ca. 1787.
   Lent by Mrs. Robert D. Chellis.

86 STUART, Gilbert (1755-1828), American
   Thomas Jefferson (1743-1826), 1805

   Aqueous grisaille on blue laid paper. H. 46.7 x 47 cm.
   Ex coll.: Thomas Jefferson (White House 1805-09; Monticello 1809-ca. 1826); his daughter, Martha Jefferson Randolph; her daughter, Ellen Wayles Randolph Coolidge, Boston; her son, Thomas Jefferson Coolidge; his daughter, Sarah Lawrence Coolidge Newbold; her son, Thomas Jefferson Newbold.
   Bibliography: Fiske Kimball, "The Life Portraits of Jefferson and their Replicas," *Proceedings of the American Philosophical Society* 88 (1944): 512-23 (ill.).
   Jules David Prown, "Medallion Life Portrait of Jefferson," *Harvard Alumni Bulletin* vol. 63 (Sept. 24, 1960): 15 (ill.).
   Alfred L. Bush, *The Life Portraits of Thomas Jefferson: Catalogue of an Exhibition at the University of Virginia Museum of Fine Arts* (Charlottesville, 1962), p. 74-77, no. 20 (ill.).
   Gift in memory of Thomas Jefferson Newbold, '10, from Mrs. Newbold and their family.   1960.156

   This portrait pleased not only Jefferson, whose interest in classical art inspired the medallion profile format, but his family and friends, who thought it an excellent likeness.

87 Jefferson, Thomas (1743-1826)
Autograph letter, signed, to Benjamin Franklin, Paris, 6 August 1787.
Ink on paper. Folded, leaf: H. 23.5 x 18.5 cm.
Lent by The Houghton Library; gift of the grandchildren of E. B. Washburne, 1927. bMS Am 1583

88 French, ca. 1790
Memorial to Benjamin Franklin: drawing for a proposed engraving
Pen and brown ink on laid paper (lower corners restored). H. 63.2 x 46.3 cm. (sight). Inscribed, on banderole, pyramid, pedestal, and medallions: tributes, mottoes, and bibliographical data (see illustration); across bottom edge, barely legible: . . . LEÉ À FAIT RÉPOSER AUX ARCHIVES NATIONALES ENTRE L'ADDRESSE À SON PRÉSIDENT ET L'EXPLICATION DES ALLÉGORIES QUE PRÉSENTE CE MAUSOLÉE COMPOSÉ ET EXÉCUTÉ À LA PLUME PAR POV . . . [or, possibly, . . . PAR ROY . . .].
Bequest of Grenville L. Winthrop. 1943.1457

Bibliography

Benjamin Franklin

Bowen, Catherine Drinker. *The Most Dangerous Man in America: Scenes from the Life of Benjamin Franklin.* Boston: Little, Brown and Co., Atlantic Monthly Press, 1974.

Cohen, I. Bernard. *Benjamin Franklin: His Contribution to the American Tradition.* Indianapolis: Bobbs-Merrill, 1953.

——— "Franklin, Benjamin." In *Dictionary of Scientific Biography*, 5:129-39. New York: Charles Scribner's Sons, 1972.

——— *Franklin and Newton: An Inquiry into Speculative Newtonian Experimental Science and Franklin's Work in Electricity as an Example Thereof.* Philadelphia: American Philosophical Society, 1956.

Franklin, Benjamin. *The Autobiography of Benjamin Franklin.* Boston and New York: Houghton Mifflin Co., 1923. (The quotations in this *Perspective* are from the 1923 edition, which may still be found in classrooms. The capitalization of nouns conforms to modern usage.)

——— *Memoirs. Parallel Text Edition.* Edited by Max Farrand. Berkeley: University of California Press, 1949. (Comprises texts of four versions of the *Autobiography*.)

——— *The Autobiography of Benjamin Franklin.* Edited by Leonard W. Labaree et al. New Haven: Yale University Press, 1964.

——— *Benjamin Franklin's Experiments: A New Edition of Franklin's Experiments and Observations on Electricity.* Edited by I. Bernard Cohen. Cambridge: Harvard University Press, 1941. (First *American* edition.)

——— *The New-England Courant: A Selection . . .* Introduction by Perry Miller. Boston: The American Academy of Arts and Sciences, 1956.

——— *The Papers of Benjamin Franklin.* Vols. 1-14, edited by Leonard W. Labaree et al. Vol. 15- , edited by William B. Willcox et al. New Haven: Yale University Press, 1959- .

——— *The Writings of Benjamin Franklin*. Edited by Albert H. Smyth. 10 vols. New York: Macmillan, 1905-07.

Fleming, Thomas, ed. *Benjamin Franklin: A Biography in His Own Words*. New York: Harper & Row, 1972.

Lane, William Coolidge. *Harvard College and Franklin, Publications of the Colonial Society of Massachusetts: Transactions*, 1904-06, 10:229-39. Boston, 1907.

Miller, Perry. *The New England Mind: From Colony to Province*. Cambridge: Harvard University Press, 1953.

Sellers, Charles Coleman. *Benjamin Franklin in Portraiture*. New Haven: Yale University Press, 1962.

Stearns, Raymond Phineas. *Science in the British Colonies of America*. Urbana: University of Illinois Press, 1970.

Van Doren, Carl. *Benjamin Franklin*. New York: Viking Press, 1938.

Artists and Artisans, Portraits and Apparatus

Cohen, I. Bernard. *Some Early Tools of American Science*. Cambridge: Harvard University Press, 1950.

Finer, Ann, and Savage, George. *The Selected Letters of Josiah Wedgwood*. New York: Born & Hawes, 1965.

Gray, John M. *James and William Tassie*. Edinburgh: Walter Greenoak Patterson, 1894.

Halsey, R. T. H.; Downs, Joseph; and Davidson, Marshall. *Benjamin Franklin and His Circle: A Catalogue of an Exhibition at the Metropolitan Museum of Art*. New York, 1936.

Huntsinger, Laura M. *Harvard Portraits: A Catalogue*. . . . Edited by Alan Burroughs. Cambridge: Harvard University Press, 1936.

Mongan, Agnes, and Wadsworth, Mary. *Exhibition: Washington, Franklin, Lafayette*. Cambridge: Harvard University: Fogg Museum of Art, February, 1944.

Prown, Jules David. *John Singleton Copley*. 2 vols. Cambridge: Harvard University Press, 1966.

Reilly, Robin, and Savage, George. *Wedgwood: The Portrait Medallions*. London: Barrie & Jenkins, 1973.

Scheidemantel, Vivian J. "Josiah Wedgwood's 'Heads of Illustrious Moderns,' Catalogue of a Special Loan Exhibition." Art Institute of Chicago, November, 1958. Reprinted in The American Wedgwoodian, 2 (1968): 156-63; 3 (1968): 14-19; 3 (1969): 42-52.

Sellers, Charles Coleman. Portraits and Miniatures by Charles Willson Peale, Transactions of the American Philosophical Society. Vol. 42, pt. 1. Philadelphia, 1952.

Storelli, A. Jean-Baptiste Nini: Sa Vie – Son Oeuvre. Tours: A. Mame et fils, 1896.

Wheatland, David P. The Apparatus of Science at Harvard, 1765-1800. Cambridge: Harvard University Press, 1968.